PAPERLESS SECURITIES

THE AUTHORS

Vadim Anatol'evich *Belov*, кандидат юридических наук, профессор is a distinguished authority on Russian civil law and the author of a major general treatise on the subject, together with volumes on the law of securities, bills of exchange, financial instruments, and others.

William Elliott *Butler*, B.A., M.A., J.D., LL.M., Ph.D., LL.D., is Professor of Comparative Law in the University of London; Director, The Vinogradoff Institute, University College London; and a senior partner in JurisPhoenix Law Firm. He is the author of numerous works on Russian and CIS legal systems, including *Russian Law* (2d ed.; Oxford University Press, 2003).

Maryann E. *Gashi-Butler*, B.A., M.A., J.D., LL.M., has been managing law firms in Moscow and elsewhere in the CIS since 1990 and is a founding and senior partner of JurisPhoenix Law Firm and founder and President of CIS Consultants Inc. She has been involved in numerous securities transactions in CIS jurisdictions.

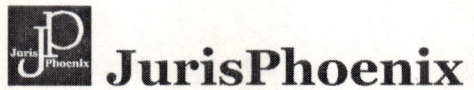

V. A. Belov

PAPERLESS SECURITIES

Third Revised Edition

———

Translated, with an Introduction, by

William E. Butler
and
Maryann E. Gashi-Butler

Wildy, Simmonds & Hill Publishers Ltd.
London
2003

Belov V.A.
Paperless Securities (A Scientific-Practical Study). – 3d ed; M.:AO
"Centre JurInfoR", 2003. 106 p.

Translation copyright © by William E. Butler and Maryann E. Gashi-
Butler, 2003
Introduction copyright © by William E. Butler and Maryann E. Gashi-
Butler, 2003
Russian text copyright © by V. A. Belov, 2003
Russian edition copyright © by АО «Центр ЮрИнфоР», 2003

British Library Cataloguing-in-Publication Data:
A catalogue record for this book is available from The British Library

I. Belov,V.A.

ISBN 1 898029 64 4

Contents

INTRODUCTION

William E. Butler and Maryann E. Gashi-Butler

THIS IS NOT an easy book. Although addressed to Russian practitioners in the legal, financial, and securities professions, it is conceptual, abstract, argumentative, even polemical and occasionally rude, uncompromisingly critical, but always stimulating, thoughtful, and, in the end, constructive. It examines that most vexsome of issues: the legal status of securities under Russian law, with special reference to so-called paperless securities.

To those western investors ready to risk the Russian securities markets – and the numbers are increasing slowly after the crash of August 1998 – the legal definition of a security is of crucial importance when assessing the legal risk associated with or arising out of an investment transaction. The early instincts of Russian legal science, following the traditions of Soviet legal science, were to attempt a generic definition of a security, or at least a generic definition of individual types of securities (stock, cheque, bill of exchange, and so on). Neither of these undertakings, as Dr. Belov observes, has proved to be efficacious; rather, they have proved to be confusing, illogical, flawed, ill-conceived, and even detrimental to the securities market as a whole.

To read Dr. Belov is akin to eavesdropping on a dialogue amongst Russian jurists and non-jurists (Philistines, to borrow the author's characterization) that has transpired during the past decade around securities legislation no less flawed than doctrinal thinking – or so the protagonists contend. The western reader might be inclined to "leave them to it", but for the fact that the debate, whatever the outcome proves to be, is in and of itself legal risk with respect to the securities market. Although the author shares a traditional perception of the sources of Russian law, and therefore considers as relevant judicial practice for the purposes of this monograph only decrees and informational letters of the Supreme Arbitrazh Court, Russian courts

viii

often find securities cases extremely challenging to resolve and may
fall back on principles fundamentally antithetical to a securities market
(as, for example, has occurred with the legal status of futures
transactions under Russian law, which unless they satisfy certain
criteria laid down by the Supreme Arbitrazh Court, may be
unenforceable in Russia because they are classified as a form of
gambling).

The present writer may be partly at fault for introducing the
expression "paperless securities" into Russian terminological currency.
At least the late Professor V. Dozortsev so contended, for we did
indeed create and use that expression in a draft general law on
securities published at Moscow in 1993.[1] The authors of that draft
law (W. E. Butler, V. Dozortsev, A. L. Makovskii) drew special
attention to the fact that:

> The draft endeavors to take into account recent trends
> connected with the modern development of social relations. It
> is well-known that in connection with the development of
> computer technology many rights personified traditionally by
> "securities" have ceased to be fixed on "paper" and are losing
> documentary form. Experience shows that the fixation of such
> rights in computer memories is sufficient and this enables the
> rights to be effectuated rather reliably and even to be alienated.
> This trend has been consolidated in a number of foreign
> legislative acts, and has received expression in Russian practice,
> in particular, connected with stocks. The Draft consolidates
> respective provisions relating to "paperless" securities.[2]

---

[1] See *Закон о ценных бумагах (Проект)* (Moscow, 1993).
(Исследовательский центр частного права. Российское Движение
Демократических Реформ). 48 p. 1500 ptd.
[2] Note 1 above, p. 3. Also see: W. E. Butler, "Draft Law of the Russian
Federation on Securities", *Butterworths Journal of Banking and
Financial Law*, VIII, no. 3 (1993), pp. 133-147, for the complete English
version of the Draft.

The approach of the Draft was both universal and tentative. The expression "paperless securities" was avoided in the text itself. Rather, Article 3 referred to the "Consolidation and Registration of Rights With Regard to Securities in Computer Memory". The Draft envisaged a scheme of specialized computer centers operating under license of a State Securities Commission. The provisions were not necessarily limited to emission securities.

This is not the occasion to resuscitate a Draft long dormant and doubtless forgotten, although it is interesting a decade on to look back to see how many problems of modern securities legislation were anticipated at the time and a proposed solution tabled for contemplation. In retrospect one wonders at the audacity and boldness of the authors of that Draft in attempting a generic law on securities, rather than individual legislation for each type of security.

Paperless securities have confounded Russian legal doctrine and practice for reasons endemic to the Soviet legal tradition and in some measure rooted in precepts of Roman Law. Russian law experiences difficulties with conceptualizing and conferring legal status on intangibles, rights, incorporeal "essences" (in the philosophical sense) as "something" that may be in ownership or possession, that may be "held", alienated, and so on, and that may be defended in a judicial or arbitral proceeding. Dr. Belov deploys the concept of "something" very astutely in his analysis of the problem. And as even the "Philistine" can see, the web of concepts, definitions, premises, assumptions, and characterizations is such in Russian legal doctrine and legislation that any ultimately accepted conception is expected to fit neatly into the procrustean bed of previously established Russian legal abstractions and categories, including procedural.

It is a particular merit of Dr. Belov's analysis that he considers the implications of various positions taken in doctrine and practice for remedies available under Russian law and judicial practice. All too often this is overlooked, and yet nothing could be more pertinent to an assessment of legal risk. A right without a remedy is legal risk of the highest order.

Investors, investment consultants, financial specialists, bankers, brokers, and the business community at large are the targeted audience of the Russian version, and our English translation is directed at the same community, together with the legal profession and auditors, outside the Russian Federation. The text will repay careful study, perhaps repeatedly, to master the definitions and assumptions that Dr. Belov makes when levelling his criticisms and assessing his concerns. One would expect to see the implications of this study reflected in securities filings in the United States and United Kingdom, for investors are plainly on notice as to the state of affairs in the law.

***

The translation follows closely the Russian terminology, style, and cadence of the text, minimizing the element of polemic where that would not be appropriate to, or would be lost upon, a foreign audience. Extracts from the Civil Code are drawn from W. E. Butler, *Civil Code of the Russian Federation* (Oxford University Press, 2003), and the text of the Federal Law on the Securities Market is reproduced from W. E. Butler, *Russian Company and Commercial Law* (Oxford University Press, 2003). For the general legal terminology used in this translation, see W. E. Butler, *Russian-English Legal Dictionary* (Dobbs Ferry, Transnational Publishers, 2001).

Chapter 1: Paperless Securities in Legislation (Unobtrusive, but Ineradicible Contradictions)

WE HAVE many reasons for writing the present work. Which of these became the "last straw" is impossible to say. On the other hand, we can with confidence point to that circumstance which for the first time awakened in us the idea of undertaking such a study. This circumstance was the glaring inconsistency, the contradictions, of two legislative norms in the Civil Code and one of the numerous special Russian laws. Legislation in force abounds with such contradictions, but one is special. Special because its subject one of the key institutions of civil law, and because, despite its obviousness and unseemliness, it is stubbornly ignored by practitioners and scholars. Here is what we have in mind.

We read the definition of the term "securities" offered to us in Article 142(1) of the Civil Code:
"A security shall be a document certifying, in compliance with the established form and obligatory requisites, property rights whose effectuation or transfer shall be possible only when presenting it", moreover "with the transfer of the security shall pass all rights in aggregate which are certified by it."

Thus, according to the Civil Code, a security is a *document*.[1]

---

[1] Even the proponents of a "broad understanding" of securities agree with this, that is. the inclusion in this concept of not only securities — documents, securities in the strict sense of the word, but also paperless securities. In general, the definition can be considered one of the central postulates of civil-law science. See V. K. Andreev, *Рынок ценных бумаг: Правовое регулирование. Курс лекций* [The Securities Market: Legal Regulation. Course of Lectures] (M., 1998). p. 25; E. A. Krasheninnikov, *Ценные бумаги на предъявителя* [Bearer Securities] (Iaroslavl, 1995), pp. 5-6; D. V. Murzin, *Ценные бумаги – бестелесные вещи. Правовые проблемы современной теории ценных бумаг* [Securities – Incorporeal Things. Legal Problems of the Contemporary Theory of Securities] (M.,

Understanding a security otherwise, the Federal Law of 22 April 1996, No. 39-ФЗ, "On the Securities Market",[2] which, in spite of its general, universal name (concerning the securities market in general, any securities) in reality relates only to *emission* securities — securities of mass issues. Article 2 of that Law commences, naturally, with the definition of the understanding of an emission security, beginning thus: "emission security — any security, including a paperless security ...".

Please note. If the definition of the term "emission security" is effectuated through the more general "security", then it is logical to suggest that the determining term should be used in the same meaning that at the moment of the adoption of the Federal Law on the Securities Market had been established by prevailing legislation. Such meaning had been established by the Civil Code: a security is a document. But suddenly there appeared a clarification: any security, including a paperless one. We hope that nobody will deny that the adjective "paperless" [*бездокументарный*] is formed in Russian from the two words: "without a document", or in Russian "*без*" "*документа*"; in other words, it means that certain property rights are certified by something, however *not a document in the hands of an empowered subject*. As very precisely expressed by contemporary scholars: "In the event of a paperless form of the issue of securities, a document having the status of a security is lacking."[3] This means, according to

---

cont'd
1998), p. 5ff.

[2] *СЗ РФ* (1996), no. 17, item 1918; (1998), no. 48. item 5857; (1999), no. 28. item 3472; (2001), no. 33(I), item 3424; (2002), no. 52(II), item 5141. Hereinafter — Federal Law on the Securities Market. For the text, see Annex 1 below.

[3] Andreev, note 1 above. p. 33. Similarly, see: A. V. Belevich. «Ценные бумаги как объекты гражданского права. Эмиссионные ценные бумаги» [Securities as the Object of Civil Rights. Emission Securities], in A. E. Sherstobitov, *Правовые основы рынка ценных бумаг* [Legal Foundations of the Securities Market]. (M., 1997), p. 75.

the Federal Law on the Securities Market, a security is something that can exist regardless of the form in which it is vested — documentary or paperless. In other words, according to the Federal Law on the Securities Market, *a security is not a document*. Or, in any event, not always a document.

How can that be? Why up to this time has the necessary attention not been given to such a glaring inconsistency of norms of the Civil Code and a Federal Law?[4] How did it turn out that the norms of both the Civil Code and the Law regulating different, as a matter of fact, institutions in practice contrive to apply to one and the same essences — stocks and bonds? And what are securities according to the Law?

We turn to Article 142(2) and Article 149 of the Civil Code of the Russian Federation.

Article 142(2) provides that "in the instances provided for by the law or in the procedure established by it in order to

---

[4] This inconsistency was mentioned by Zh. V. Korshunova, «Правовой режим безбумажных ценных бумаг», [The Legal Regime of Paperless Securities"], in *Актуальные проблемы науки и практики коммерческого права: сборник научных трудов* [Urgent Problems of Science and the Practice of Commercial Law: Collection of Scientific Works] (Spb., 2000), p. 54; however, considering such a situation impossible, she brushes it off almost with an exclamation "get away from me" and proclaims that a person who sees such an inconsistency does not understand the meaning of the Federal Law on the Securities Market. Behaving similarly are M. Krylova, «Ценная бумага – вещь, документ или совокупность прав» [A Security — Thing, Document or Aggregate of Rights?], *Рынок ценных бумаг* [Securities Market], no. 2 (1997), p. 60; and I. Lysikhin, «Давайте разберемся в дефинициях» [Let's Analyze the Definitions], *Рынок ценных бумаг* [The Securities Market], no. 17 (1996), p. 37: recognizing that the Civil Code in reality defines a security as a document, they declare the root of evil to be the definition in the Civil Code! Not that the Federal Law on the Securities Market has come to contradict the Civil Code, but the Civil Code — the Law! This, excuse me, is all the same as writing: "the adopted Law does not contradict practice". What's the difference? The question should be otherwise: is not practice contrary to the law?

effectuate and transfer the *rights*, certified by *a security, evidence of its being consolidated in a special register (ordinary or computerized)* **shall be sufficient**. At present the discussion concerns only the fact that sometimes (in instances provided by a law or in the procedure established by it) for the effectuation and transfer of rights certified by a security (i.e. a document), *it is not necessary to present the document*; it is sufficient that these same rights embodied in the security-document, would be at the same time fixed in a special register — a special document which is maintained either by the same emittent or on its behalf by a third person. The Civil Code made a mistake of principle: infringing on the holy of holies of the theory of securities — the principle of the presentation of a security as a condition necessary for the effectuation and transfer of rights in it and from it.[5]

Having severed the principle of presentation, the Civil Code should have made the sole logical conclusion arising from that fact: as soon as there are instances when the presentation of a document is not necessary, this means *it is possible to reject the very idea of the existence of such a document as a security*, having made, as the sole condition of its existence, the effectuation and the transfer of rights which *would be* embodied in the security *the consolidation of such in a special register*.[6] Article 149 of the Civil Code is dedicated to the implementation of this idea, in accordance with point 1 of which the rights which *would be certified* by the securities could be certified otherwise, namely by of the fulfillment of respective

[5] However, not all authors agree with this. Korshunova "suggests that" presentability is characteristic not only of documentary but of paperless securities (note 4 above, p. 58). Naturally, in order to substantiate that thesis it was necessary for her to compose a definition of presentation (note 4 above, p. 59) that would not yield, as one Russian civilist wrote, "either to commentary, or even to comprehension".

[6] See: V. Speranskii, «Бездокументарные ценные бумаги» [Paperless Securities], *Российская юстиция* [Russian Justice], no. 4 (1998). The relevant text is contained in Data Base "Garant-Maksimum."

entries concerning those rights by a person who has obtained a special license. To be sure, two substantive provisos have been made here: the particular rule can work only (1) in instances determined by a law or in the procedure established by it; (2) with regard to rights consolidated by an inscribed or order security. Accordingly, all operations with such rights (as referred to in Article 149(2) of the Civil Code — "with paperless securities") "... may be performed only by having recourse to the person who has officially performed the entry of the rights. The transfer, granting and limitation of rights must be officially fixed by this person, who shall bear responsibility for the preservation of the official entries, ensuring their confidentiality, submission of correct data concerning such entries. and the performance of official records concerning operations carried on".

In other respects, to paperless securities "...the rules established for securities shall apply ... unless it arises otherwise from the peculiarities of the fixation" (Article 149(1), Civil Code).

Here is the basis on which is constructed the concept of a security in the Federal Law on the Securities Market. The vulgarisation of the approach used by the Civil Code – that is, how the method could be labelled which was applied when drawing up the Federal Law on the Securities Market.[7] We compare the theses of the Civil Code and the Law.

In the Civil Code it is said: securities exist — presentation and publicly reliable *documents* certifying property rights are necessary. However, sometimes such rights may be certified by other means than by the issuance of such documents — by the drawing up and making of necessary changeable and publicly reliable *entries concerning property rights*, their content, volume and dynamics. Insofar as the goal of this method of certifying rights is the replacement of the securities

---

[7] And likewise — Murzin, suggesting that Article 142(2) of the Civil Code gives a definition of paperless securities (note 1 above, p. 12).

(the documents), the rights certified in such manner are subordinated to the rules concerning the rights certified by securities.

The Law decreed: securities exist — something that can be embodied both in the form of a solitary document, issued into the hands of an empowered person, or by an entry in a special register. In so far as in one case or the other, the "something" is a security, the rules on securities apply. According to the Federal Law on the Securities Market, securities are understood to be the *aggregate of property rights*, but by no means a document fixing these rights. Especially significant in this context is Article 16(6) of the Law, establishing that "Any property and nonproperty rights consolidated in documentary or paperless form irrespective of their name are emission securities ..."[8] and the name of Article 18 of the Law ("Form of *Certification of Rights Comprising Emission Security*").[9]

---

[8] Korshunova affirms that in the given formulation the legislator wanted only to focus attention on the fact that the nature of the value of a security is rooted precisely in the aggregate of rights (note 4 above, p. 54), but this is not at all what he said. In the first place, the conclusion that the Federal Law on the Securities Market understands by the term securities precisely property rights follows literally from all of its provisions, and not only from the said norm of Article 16, and in the second place, it is not understandable why the legislator preferred to substitute himself as the teacher and instead of establishing a legal norm ("if before us is the aggregate of rights meeting some kind of indicia, then these rights are a security, and the status of the holder of those rights is determined by the present Law"), communicated a generally known truth of economic science contentious to nobody. In any event, the argument "I suggest that" on which the author substantiated her opinion is manifestly inadequate. To the point, literally on the following page of her immortal work (note 4 above, p. 55) the supplicant Korshunova again relies on the quoted norm of Article 16 of the Law, but not as an object of criticism but as an argument in favour of one of the many absurd propositions advanced by her. Simply a model of unfair polemics.

[9] Lysikhin provides us with some interesting information: "In one of the

Being objective, one can not fail to note that such vulgarisation in no small degree was facilitated by the compilers of the Civil Code themselves. Thus, in Article 149(1), paragraph one, the concept of the paperless form of fixing rights is deciphered as the fixing "... (with the assistance of electronic-computer technology, and the like)", i.e., as fixing effectuated without the use of any, in general, traditional (composed on a paper carrier) document. The paper register, according to Article 149(1), paragraph one, of the Civil Code, is therefore the normal, documentary form of fixing rights. Absurd? Undoubtedly. And although already in Article 149(1), paragraph two, and (2), the term "paperless securities" is used much more broadly — now encompassing any form of the fixing of rights which is not accompanied by the issuance into the hands of an empowered person a classical security — a document, the ambiguity of Article 149(1), paragraph one, has served its purpose: in practice there appeared issues of "documentary" securities, formalized as "global certificates,"[10] and in the Federal Law on the Securities Market appeared the concept "securities in documentary form with obligatory centralized keeping".

cont'd
variants of the Law in 1994, the term "security" was introduced as "an indivisible aggregate of property rights ...". In the opinion of the drafters of the law, this definition more fully reflected the concept of "a security"; however it did not find its way into the final draft of the law since it contradicted the definition of security in the Civil Code as adopted at that time." (Lysikhin, note 4 above, pp. 37-38). An analogous definition from the draft law «Об инвестиционных ценных бумагах и фондовых биржах» [On Investment Securities and the Stock Exchanges], *Экономика и жизнь* [The Economy and Life: Your Partner], no. 44 (1994), p. 16) we also quoted in our monograph of 1996 (p. 128). They removed the definition, but its "ears" remained to stick out from almost every norm of the Law!
[10] "A Global Certificate"—a documentary form of issuance of securities ... At the same time the circulation of the securities certified by them takes place just as do paperless." (Lysikhin, note 4 above, p. 40).

Further. In speaking in Article 149(1), paragraph one, about the paperless *form* of fixing rights and about the fact that the rules concerning securities apply precisely to that *form* of fixing rights (and not to the rights themselves), the Civil Code gave occasion for the interpretation thereof in the sense that *by paperless securities is understood* the very form of fixing property rights, i.e. the *entry in the register* (either ordinary or computerized).[11] Such an interpretation has all the more grounds since in subsequent norms of this same Article the term "paperless form" was replaced with "paperless securities." The result achieved was terrible: the draftsmen of the Federal Law on the Securities Market, having forgotten their basic postulate (that any security is an aggregate of rights), began to use expressions, of the type "rights consolidated by a security", "rights in securities", "rights with regard to securities" (Articles 2, 18, 28, 29, and others). All these expressions in the context of the Law make sense only when securities are understood as something distinct from the document and the property rights consolidated by it, i.e., for example, the *entries of the person effectuating the fixing of the rights*. But this, of course, is an obvious absurdity. No stockholder has any kind of rights to any part of the register or entry from it. The very register — be it a document in paper or magnetic carrier form — is in the ownership of the person who is engaged in keeping it and this right of ownership is not encumbered by any rights of third persons. Accordingly, to establish or transfer a right to an entry in a register is as impossible, as it is nonsensical. "The method of fixation can not be an object of civil-law relations…",[12] Iuldashbaeva points

---

[11] This proposition was defended by V. I. Iakovlev under my scholarly supervision. See V. I. Iakovlev, *Регулятивные и охранительные правоотношения в сфере рынка ценных бумаг в России* [Regulatory and Protective Legal Relations in the Sphere of the Securities Market in Russia] (M., 1999), pp. 6, 9-12. (Dissertation abstract: канд. юридических наук).

[12] L. R. Iuldashbaeva , *Правовое регулирование оборота эмиссионных*

out. This is one of the few indisputably just propositions of her monograph.

In no small measure, the views of the majority of "contemporary scholars" have encouraged the softening of the mentioned inconsistency, striving not so much to help practice adequately to explain (or to interpret) the illiterately drafted legislation, but to pass off as their own "theories" the existing legislative constructions. It is natural that the absurdity of the latter lay with the indelible birthmarks on the first, concerning which we[13] and certain other civilists[14] already

cont'd

ценных бумаг [Legal Regulation of the Circulation of Emission Securities (Stocks, Bonds)]. (M., 1999), p. 37.

[13] See the following of our works: V. A. Belov, «О безналичной форме выпуска ценных бумаг» [Concerning the Cashless Form of Issuance of Securities], Бизнес и банки [Business and Banks], no. 35 (1993), p. 5; id, Ценные бумаги в российском гражданском праве [Securities in Russian Civil Law] (M., 1996), pp. 123-140; id, Ценных бумаги как объекты гражданских прав: Вопросы теории [Securities as Objects of Civil Rights: Questions of Theory. Dissertation…Kand. Iuridicheskii Nauk in the form of a scholarly report, fulfilling the function also of an abstract] (M., 1996), pp. 20-26; id, «Юридическая природа 'бездокументарных ценных бумаг' и 'безналичных денежных средств'» [The Legal Nature of "Paperless Securities" and "Noncash Monetary Means" in Рынок ценных бумаг [The Securities Market], no. 5 (1997), pp. 23-26; no. 6, pp. 49-52; «Комментарий к статье И. Горбикаева и Ю. Баранова 'Как защитить права собственников именных ценных бумаг'» [Commentary to the article of I. Gorbikov and Iu. Baranov, How to Defend Rights of Owners of Bearer Securities in The Securities Market]. No. 13 (1997), p. 95; id, «Защита интересов добросовестного приобретателя ценной бумаги» [The Defence of Interests of the Good Faith Acquirer of Securities], Законодательство [Legislation], no. 6 (1997), pp. 33-39.

[14] See, for example: Krasheninnikov, note 1 above, p. 7, including the footnote; pp. 11-12; E. A. Sukhanov, «Вступительная статья» у Belov, Ценные бумаги в российском гражданском праве [Introductory article to our book Securities in Russian Civil Law] (M., 1996), pp. 4-5, 9-10, 12-15, and others.

had the honour to speak about in print. We will not repeat them here; merely briefly summarize the substance of the discussion at the present moment.

There is no doubt that the nature of the "value" of securities consists not of the natural properties of documents, but in the subjective civil rights certified by them.[15] However, from this it does not follow at all that securities, considered as objects of civil-law relations, are directly property rights.[16] This does not necessarily follow at all. If the particular rights are embodied in a publicly reliable document, with the affiliation of which as things the affiliation of the rights are connected certified by this document, the object of civil rights becomes this *document* itself, the classical security, i.e. *a thing*. If the particular rights do not have such embodiment, but have been fixed in a register of a specialized registrar, then they, from the point of view of theory of objects of legal relations, remain *merely property rights*.

The terminology should also be conforming. If we speak of securities in the economic sense of the word, then, of course, it is possible to combine under this term both documents and rights.[17] If we speak about *securities* as objects of civil-law

---

[15] According to legislation, certainly property [rights], although from the point of view of theory and practice such a "self-limitation" is not necessary, and besides, not in conformity with reality.

[16] This is confirmed, for example, by Trusova, declaring that "from the point of view of legal nature, securities are property rights". O. A. Trusova, «Некоторые вопросы правового регулирования залога ценных бумаг» [Some Questions of the Legal Regulation of the Pledge of Securities], in *Актуальные проблемы науки и практики коммерческого права: Сборник научных трудов* [Urgent Problems of Science and the Practice of Commercial Law: Collection of Scientific Works] (Spb., 2000), III, p. 97. Economic, yes; legal — on no account. The same author two pages earlier specially stipulated that a security in her article is a document, and only a document, and so far as it is a document, it is a thing. And there is the "legal nature"! What other "legal nature" the author wants to find — to us, we confess, is unclear.

[17] It is similar to how economists under "money" combine money proper,

relations, then by them it is possible to understand *only documents*, and not subjective civil rights embodied in them. As expressed by Marchenko, the essence and value of a security are the rights, but is itself a thing itself "symbolizing a certain complex of rights."[18] Or, otherwise, in the terminology of Trusova, "... the relegation of the security to things corresponds to the definition of a security as a document".[19]

In turn, it follows that *paperless securities* should be understood as the *property rights themselves* (documentary theory).

The combining of rights,[20] obligations,[21] certain "incorporeal (nonmaterial) things",[22] "(symbols of) complexes of rights",[23] "abstract things",[24] "aggregate of rights",[25]

---

cont'd

banknotes, money surrogates, other tokens of value, and even rights of demand to contributions, deposits and accounts.

[18] See A. Marchenko «Символ комплекса прав» [Symbol of a Complex of Rights], *Рынок ценных бумаг* [The Securities Market], no. 12 (1996), p.14.

[19] Trusova, note 16 above, p. 95.

[20] "A security as an incorporeal thing — is a contractual right of obligation regulated by the norms of a right to a thing." (Murzin, note 1 above, p. 79). The given definition relates to something fictional, fantastic, because the rights of obligations are not subordinate to the norms of a right to a thing. See also: Speranskii, note 6 above; Iuldashbaeva, note 12 abpve, pp. 37, 57, 66 and others.

[21] "... A security can be characterized as an obligation between the person who issued it and the subject of the rights certified by this security, its possessor" (Andreev, note 1 above, p. 29). It is possible, but not necessary, as this characteristic rarely is empty. If a security is an obligation, then who is "the subject of the rights certified by the obligation"? How can it in general be — so that the obligation (legal relation, essence, formed from the right and obligation) certified someone's rights?

[22] Krylova, note 4 above, pp. 29, 31; Murzin, note 1 above, pp. 78-79.

[23] Marchenko, note 18 above, p. 14.

[24] Marchenko, note 18 above, p. 14.

[25] Krylova, note 4 above,, pp. 29, 31; Lysikhin, note 4 above, pp. 37-38 and others.

"fictions" (subjective-rights theory)[26] under the term "securities", together with the publicly reliable, presentation, and negotiable documents is based on a lack of understanding of that obvious circumstance *that is objectively not possible to subject objects of the material world, things (documents) and things ideal (rights and "symbols") to identical legal regulation, to impart to them the same legal regime.*[27] If any rules on securities extend to paperless securities, then this does not mean that paperless securities are a type of securities, precisely just as if certain rules on cats are extended to dogs, it does not mean that dogs are a breed (or species) of cat. "It would be incorrect to consider that the means of equating (personification) by the legislator means complete identity".[28]

---

[26] E.S. Demushkina, «Безналичные ценные бумаги – фикция или реальность» [Non-Cash Securities — Fiction or Reality?], *Рынок ценных бумаг* [The Securities Market], no. 20 (1996), p. 68; L. Efimova, «Правовой режим бездокументарных ценных бумаг» [The Legal Regime of Paperless Securities], *Закон* [Law], no. 7 (1997), p. 53; id, «Правовые проблемы бехналичных денег» [Legal Problems of Non-Cash Securities", *Хозяйство и право* [The Economy and Law], no. 2 (1997), p. 45.

[27] It is impossible not to mention examples of the lack of understanding of this circumstance in the debates of the majority of contemporary scholar-innovators. The general leit-motiv, the best of all which was formulated (true, as applied to the so-called non-cash money) was by Demushkina, approximately as follows: "the absence of a "classical" material carrier itself where there are present legislatively consolidated "substitutes" … can not, in my view, be considered in and of itself as a hindrance to the regulation of non-cash monetary means with the norms of [a right to a thing.]" (Demushkina, note 26 above, p. 70). In brief: the legislator said "the right of ownership" — means "the right of ownership." Further (p. 71) the author even speaks ironically about those, who build all their conclusions on the distinction of the legal regime of securities and paperless securities only on the fact of the absence of a material carrier. In vain! Alone this argument can not possibly kill a thousand others. Analogously, see: Korshunova, note 4 above, p. 55.

[28] Iuldashbaeva, note 12 above, p. 49.

A remarkable illustration of this thesis is given by Trusova using as an example the norms concerning the pledge of stocks. Considering the norms of the pledge of things and rights, she concludes that "... the pledge of securities must be effectuated according to the rules of the pledge of a thing, and the pledge of paperless securities according to the rules of pledge of a property right".[29]

At the end of her article, Krylova attempts to return to an objective analysis of the status of things. At the outset she recognizes that with respect to paperless securities, the "terminology of the right to a thing in its customary understanding"[30] is not applicable, thereupon she agrees with the necessity of the distinction between securities in the broad and narrow sense of the word, understanding under the latter namely paper publicly reliable, presentable, circulable document,[31] and, finally, gives as examples norms applicable to documentary securities, but not operative in cases of paperless securities — Articles 145, 146, 234, 327 of the Civil Code; Chapter 34 of the 2002 Code of Civil Procedure of the Russian Federation,[32] i.e. arriving at our initial thesis. Securities and paperless securities have a *different legal regime*, and this means—they are *different objects of civil law relations*.

All common sense has not been abandoned in the discourse of Murzin — the author of the first monograph in Russia, voluminous, but of little substance, on paperless securities, representing a medley of positions of classical science and pseudoscientific research. On completely just premises — a security is a document, and a right — merely content filling the security (the document) with value, he draws a correct conclusion: "... the sole indicator connecting the ordinary and paperless security is the property right certified by the

---

[29] Trusova, note 16 above, p. 101.
[30] Krylova, note 4 above, p. 31.
[31] Krylova, note 4 above, pp. 31, 32.
[32] Krylova, note 4 above, p. 32.

security."[33] Such result of a search for a unifying principle in his own words, "should be acknowledged as negative; a single definition [more accurately, concept – *V. B.*] is broken up into two diametrically opposed blocks"[34], i.e. into documents (securities) and rights (paperless). How is it possible after this to insist that "a security is an incorporeal thing"? It seems that it is possible: one need only prove that the indicia of paperless do not conform to the indicia of classical securities. Naturally, they do not conform and there is nothing to prove; yet there is one more reason for the separation of the lambs from the goats. Murzin demonstrates the miracles of logical thinking; since they do not confirm, he concludes, and since in legislation the given construction is designated as securities, it means ... classical theory is incorrect! In his opinion, by this circumstance also is explained "the resistance of [legal] science to paperless securities".[35]

It is comforting that our position is shared by the well-known St. Petersburg civilist, Drobyshev. With regard to the results of the discourse concerning the concept and nature of the paperless bill of exchange, he concluded that the paperless bill of exchange — "This is another object of civil law similar to the traditional bill of exchange *only* with respect to the content of the respective obligation."[36] We must acknowledge that Drobyshev — hardly the only scholar who has agreed that the content of an obligation — is such "only"; that the center of gravity is not in the content of rights, but in the *form in which the rights are embodied.* Those who consider otherwise, who "...do not see the conditional character of the

---

[33] Murzin, note 1 above, p. 12.
[34] Murzin, note 1 above, p. 19.
[35] Murzin, note 1 above, p. 31.
[36] P. Iu. Drobyshev, «Бездокументарный вексель: юридическая конструкция и право на сосуществование» [Paperless Bill of Exchange: Juridical Construction and the Right to Exist], *Рынок ценных бумаг* [The Securities Market], no. 17 (1996), p. 48.

name and specific character of the juridical construction..., make a flagrant mistake".[37]

What efforts have been made by scholars to reconcile the Federal Law on Securities with theory can be seen in the example of recent changes in the Federal Law on Securities. From 4 January 2003, according to Article 16(1) of the said Law in the new version "inscribed emission securities may be issued only in paperless form, except for instances provided for by federal laws". Thus, in essence, the *existence of "classical" ("documentary") inscribed emission securities is prohibited,* which is contrary to the Civil Code (see Article 142(1) and Article 143). Especially urgent is the prohibition for *stocks*: against the background of the prescription that stocks may *only be inscribed* (Article 2(2), Federal Law on Securities), the norm concerning the possibility of the existence of inscribed emission securities *only in paperless form* means the *impossibility of the existence of classical documentary stocks.* The treasured wish of the legislator to deprive stocks of the status of securities, having transformed them into the "indivisible aggregate of rights of a stockholder", finally (after more than a decade of effort)[38] happened: *stocks* de facto

---

[37] Drobyshev, note 36 above, p. 49.

[38] The first step towards paperless securities was made by Section X of Statute No. 601, which authorized certificates thereof to be issued instead of stocks; next, point 1 of Statute No. 78, which decreed the possibility of the existence of securities "in the form ... of entries in accounts"; the next step was made by the Statute on the Procedure for the Payment of Dividends on Stocks and interest on bonds, confirmed by the Ministry of Economy and Finances of the Russian Federation on 10 January 1992. See Финансовая газета, no. 4 (1992), which limited the right to a dividend by the time of acquisition of the stocks (point 11); and, actually permitted dividends to be paid according to the data of the stockholder register without the presentation of stocks; finally, the penultimate step towards excluding stocks from among securities was made by the joint-stock society law, which established that the rights to a dividend and participation in the general meeting of stockholders (later – also the

ceased to be securities. The few existing issues of "documentary stocks are now considered to be paperless issues, and stocks in hand (in the expression of the Federal Law on Securities – "certificates of stocks") are "equated to extracts from the register of possessors" (Article 2(1), Federal Law on Securities as amended).

The 2003 version of the Federal Law on Securities continues the course of emasculating the concept of emission bearer securities (only bonds may be such). However, having in view the relatively narrow range of the practice of issuing bonds in general, one may imagine the quantity of bearer bonds to be minimal. Now a blow has been inflicted not only against *bearer bonds*, but against *bearer securities as a whole.* Article 16, paragraph five, of the Federal Law on Securities has established that "By decision concerning the issue of bearer emission securities ... it may be determined that such securities are subject to obligatory centralised keeping). A certificate of bearer emission securities with obligatory centralised keeping may not be issued by hand to the possessor(s) of such securities". The bearer of what, in this instance, is the creditor under the security? To whom will this "something" be presented? How in general does one effectuate the rights from a bearer security that is not in the hands of the creditor?

----

cont'd
preferential right to acquire additional stocks) shall be effectuated not by the owner of the stocks, but ... by persons included on special Lists. Stocks as securities gradually were made into a purely nominal concept having no legal significance. Statute No. 601 is translated in W. E. Butler, *Basic Legal Documents of the Russian Federation* (1992), pp. 209-225.

Chapter 2: Paperless Securities in Judicial Practice

SECURITIES ARE documents. Paperless securities are not documents. Consequently, paperless securities are not securities. It is necessary to work somewhat to refute the simple categorical syllogism. Practice, however, does not undertake to assume such a task — desperately needed. We almost never hear the said syllogism from the mouths of practitioners; substantiation of the fact that paperless securities are securities is coming down, for example, to the following: since in the term "paperless securities" the word "securities" figures, it follows that paperless securities are securities. Consider an example of analogous reasoning: since in the phrase "liquid stool" (diarrhea) the word "stool" figures, this means that "liquid stool" is a variety of chair.

It would not be superfluous to turn one's attention to the internal inconsistencies of the Federal Law on Securities and the Civil Code mentioned above. If according to the legislation paperless securities are rights, recordings, something more (like an incorporeal thing), "where there is a maiden, so to speak, there is a vision", then it is necessary to understand on which of these many views practice has settled and why. If paperless securities are rights, then the rules of their ownership, effectuation, change of person are defined by the norms of the Civil Code on *legal capacity, dispositive legal capacity,* and *legal succession.* If paperless securities are something incorporeal, but not coinciding with subjective rights, then *a construction of a special absolute right* in this very "incorporeal something" is necessary, or the rights of ownership in the incorporeal, including in the right, cannot be. In any case, should not be.

A directly contrary conclusion follows from the norms of Article 2(14) and Articles 28 and 29 of the Federal Law on the Securities Market dealing with the category "right to a security", including in paperless securities, implying under that term "the right of ownership" or "other right to a thing." The most zealous proponents of the theories quoting these and similar norms continue to find their basis even in the norms of the 1991 Fundamental Principles of Civil Legislation of the USSR and Republics and in the Civil Code. Thus, Article 4(1) of the Fundamental Principles and Article 128(1) of the Civil Code establish that, apart from traditional things (including money and securities), *"other property, including property rights"* relate to objects of civil rights. From the cited formulation they conclude that the Fundamental Principles and the Civil Code include in the concept "property" three different concepts: "things" (in the true sense of the word, money and securities), "property rights" and "other property." That *all property rights are property* is an important conclusion following from these formulations. Paperless securities are either things or a variety of property rights. Consequently, irrespective of from what aspect they are regarded, *paperless securities under any variant are property*.

An object of the right of ownership is *property* according to Articles 44 and 45 of the 1991 Fundamental Principles and Article 209 of the Civil Code. In so far as all paperless securities are property and any property may be an object of the right of ownership, consequently *paperless securities may be in someone's ownership*.[39]

To even the least literate lawyer the mistake in this discourse is obvious. The use of one and the same term in different meanings does not allow one to put the other meaning in the same context. But exactly this is being done by those who wish to substantiate the right of ownership to rights; in Article 209 of the Civil Code instead of the term "property" they place it under that meaning in which it was used in Article 128. However, the term "property" has many meanings (it is sufficient to look at any text book on civil law to be convinced

---

[39] See Korshunova, note 4 above, p. 57; Murzin, note 1 above, pp. 90-91.

of this) and in Article 209 it is used in quite another, narrower, meaning, as a synonym for the term "thing." If this was unknown to the above "substituters" a complaint should be made about their legal education; if it was known, then we should turn away in contempt from them, as one would from opponents using prohibited methods of scientific polemic.

Speaking out in favour of the extension of the right of ownership to paperless securities are Korshunova,[40] Murzin[41] and the majority of practitioners — Konovalov,[42] Kotov,[43]

---

[40] See Korshunova, note 4 above, pp. 56-57, 59. The opinion is based mainly on the provisions of legislation, decreeing that particular transactions which can be concluded with things (purchase-sale, pledge, trust management and the like) can be concluded likewise with securities and even with rights; since it is not said precisely with which — it means including paperless securities. In reality, this means nothing since the Civil Code, once again, has very precisely separated "securities" and "paperless securities"; perhaps in the absence of such a terminological distinction one might reproach the Law, but the Civil Code, in no way. This means that when the Civil Code speaks of "securities", it has in view Article 142(1); and only when it speaks of "rights" – has in view paperless securities too. However, use of words of the type "sale of a right" is merely of an exemplary character; to derive from this that rights are objects of the right of ownership is erroneous. The legislator speaks merely about the fact the assignment of a right for money is subordinated to the rules on purchase-sale.

[41] See Murzin, note 1 above, pp. 79-81, 85-87, 90-98, and following. The argumentation is the said as the preceding author, plus the postulate not corresponding to reality and unproved by the author that paperless securities – are things.

[42] See V Konovalov, «Об ответственности специализированного регистратора» [On the Responsibility of a Specialized Registrar], *Рынок ценных бумаг* [The Securities Market], no. 3 (1998), p. 33.

[43] See O. Kotov, «Сделки с акциями на внебиржевом рынке: проблемные вопросы» [Stock Transactions on the Over the Counter Market: Problem Issues], *Рынок ценных бумаг* [The Securities Market], no. 9 (1998), p. 72ff.

and Ryzhkov.[44] One should have in view that although all the aforementioned and certain other authors use legislative terms and expressions (of the type "possessor of paperless security", "purchase-sale of paperless security"), this circumstance in and of itself does not mean that they are ready to subject these expression to scholarly investigation and support the category of "right of ownership to paperless securities". Trusova, for example, behaves thus:[45] without recourse to silly legislative terminology, she in essence opposes extending the norms of the right to a thing to paperless securities; in one place she expressly says that the category of "the right of ownership to a paperless security" makes no sense in and of itself.[46] Also "against" extending the regime of rights to a thing to paperless securities are (besides us) V. V. Vitrianskii, L. A. Novoselova, E. A. Sukhanov, V. I. Chubarov, L. R. Iuldashbaeva, and others.[47] As regards practitioners, this view is shared only by Marchenko, Speranskii, and A. Shatalov – but hardly in the most categorical expressions:

> (*Marchenko*): "*For paperless securities everything may be formulated in the terms of the right of obligation.* This leads to various definitions and laws for documentary securities";[48]

---

[44] O. Ryzhkov, «Выпуск ценных бумаг: сначала права, затем бумаги» [Issue of Securities: First the Right, Next the Security], *Рынок ценных бумаг* [The Securities Market], no. 17 (1996), p. 53.

[45] See Trusova, note 16 above, pp. 96-97.

[46] Trusova, note 16 above, pp. 99, 100, 102ff.

[47] References to the sources the reader will find in works by Demushkina, Korshunova, Murzin, and Iuldashbaeva. Also see: A. Trofimenko, «Признаки ценной бумаги» [Indicia of a Security], *Российская юстиция* [Russian Justice], no. 7 (1997); id, «Споры о ценных бумагах» [Disputes Concerning Securities], *Российская юстиция* [Russian Justice], no. 6 (1998). The texts in Data Base "Garant Maksimum" have been used.

[48] Marchenko, note 18 above, p. 14.

(*Speranskii*): "Even if we allow that the rules concerning securities may be applied to the fixation of rights, *no filling-in application can legalize the application to property rights*, even though objectively fixed in a special register, *of general provisions of civil law concerning ownership and other rights to a thing*;[49]

(*Shatalov*): "The uniqueness of the situation is that *despite the character of rights to a thing declared by a law of the rights to paperless securities, in fct such rights are not rights to a thing at all* because they have not been secured by the means of defence of rights to a thing".[50]

The position formulated by Krylova is a particular one. In principle she concurs that the classical security is a thing.[51] However, in her view, this in reality is not so; "securities are documents" and were transformed into "securities – things" artificially.[52] Strange that Krylova has not developed her views to the end: she would be forced to acknowledge that not only paperless, but also documentary, securities should not subordinate themselves to norms concerning the right of ownership. Yes, by their legal regime securities stand out materially from other things, but having been placed on a base of affiliation and alienability in common with things – the right of ownership and other rights to a thing – they stand out not so as to cease being considered things in the legal, of course, sense of the word.[53]

---

[49] Speranskii, note 6 above.

[50] A. Shatalov, Как защитить права на бездокументарные ценные бумаги [How to Defend Rights to Paperless Securities], *Рынок ценных бумаг* [The Securities Market], no. 20 (1996), p. 66.

[51] Krylova, note 4 above, p. 61.

[52] Krylova, note 4 above, p. 61.

[53] The reservation that from the economic point of view securities are not, of course, things, but are valued by virtue of social and not natural properties won by man, would be superfluous. At the same time, having in view that our opponents are among the most troublesome, we in any event, not to give grounds for a baseless reproach of having done a partisan study, all the same have made this reservation.

But, enough of diversions; we return to judicial practice. The Survey of Practice of the Settlement of Disputes with regard to Transactions Connected with the Placement and Circulation of Stocks, confirmed by Information Letter of the Presidium of the Supreme Arbitrazh Court of the Russian Federation (point 7), of 21 April 1998, No. 33, indicated that the *"demand* of an owner (or person empowered by the owner) *concerning the return of stocks* presented to a good-faith acquirer is *of a vindicatio character* and may be satisfied only when there are the conditions present provided for by Article 302 of the Civil Code of the Russian Federation".[54] And although the document does not expressly say that it refers to paperless securities, nonetheless this is virtually beyond doubt since documentary stocks are rarely encountered in modern practice.

If our assumption is correct, this point of the Survey of Practice of the Presidium of the Supreme Arbitrazh Court of the RF may be interpreted in two ways: paperless securities are (1) something that *may be the subject of vindicatio* and, consequently, an *object of the right of ownership*; and (2) something to which norms concerning the conditions of satisfaction of a *vindicatio* suit may be applied *by analogy* and, respectively, norms concerning the right of ownership. The second interpretation is undoubtedly correct, but since in order to approach it one must know what is such right of ownership and for precisely which objects may it be established, a certain educational qualification is required which the majority of our fellow citizens lack and practitioners have not even noted it; all as one have latched on to the first variant of the interpretation. The substantiation of this step has been confirmed by Article 2 of the Federal Law on the Securities Market already mentioned, by which the possessor of a security (any, and consequently, also a paperless security) is a "...

---

[54] *Вестник Высшего арбитражного суда РФ*, no. 6 (1998).

person to whom securities belong *by right of ownership or other right to a thing*".

This interpretation rapidly received new confirmation by Decree of the Presidium of the Supreme Arbitrazh Court of the Russian Federation of 28 December 1999, No. 1293/99, with regard to a dispute between ZAO "Sib-Khormelinvest" and OAO "Spetsializirovannyi Registrator 'Alpari'" concerning the deeming to be illegal the withdrawal by the last of paperless securities from the personal account of the plaintiff and "... the duty to perform an operation with regard to restoring to the personal account of the plaintiff in the stockholder register a registration entry concerning the possession of the said stocks by right of ownership".[55] It would seem that any arbitrazh court, the more so the Presidium of the Supreme Arbitrazh Court, consists of specialists having a higher legal education and who know very well that the right of ownership to rights, fictions, and other incorporeal (or ideal) substances does not exist. Nonetheless, the Presidium seriously discussed the question of satisfying the suit and came to the conclusion that "the demand of a plaintiff concerning the restoration of an entry in his account *concerning the possession of the contested stocks by right of ownership* by means of withdrawal from the account of *a new illegal owner* actually comes down to a demand concerning the return of the stocks ... This demand is *of a vindicatio character* and is subject to consideration in accordance with Article 302 of the Civil Code of the Russian Federation. Whereas the interpretation of point 7 of the Survey left some doubt and contained occasion for ambiguity, here these had disappeared: paperless stocks (just as other paperless securities) are *objects of the right of ownership*.

How can a demand of an "owner" against an "illegal owner" be *vindicatio*?[56] How can it happen in general that

---

[55] *Вестник Высшего Арбитражного Суда РФ*, no. 4 (2000).
[56] This question has been brilliantly discussed by Shatalov, note 50 above, p. 66.

two rights of ownership – "legal" and "illegal" – exist to one
and the same thing? And what, in general, is an "illegal right"?
How is it possible to possess something incorporeal – something
impossible to touch and, consequently, impossible to perform
any actual actions comprising the essence of possession?[57] How
is it possible to "vindicate" that which is not a thing?, the more
so, an individually-determined thing?[58] Questions may be put
endlessly, but a fact remains a fact: despite sound reason,
despite the norms of the Civil Code of the Russian Federation,
irrespective of the postulates of legal science, legislation, and
then – law enforcement practice too:

(1) from the outset refused to classify securities as
documents and deemed such to be the aggregate of rights;

(2) next deemed paperless securities – fixed in a special
register of the right – to be "incorporeal rights", which
led

(3) to paperless securities being considered as objects of
the right of ownership, a subject of *vindicatio*, a subject
of traditional general civil-law contracts directed

---

[57] Although, if one is guided by the position of Murzin and Korshunova,
who regard the essence of the possession of property as the "entry on the
balance sheet" (Murzin, note 1 above, p. 89; Korshunova, note 4 above,
pp. 57-58), then undoubtedly it is possible. How I want to see a citizen on
"whose balance sheet" Murzin and Korshunova propose to enter the
stock.

[58] Gorbikov and Baranov put this question to themselves. See I. Gorbikov
and Iu. Baranov, «Как защитить права собственности именных
ценных бумаг» [How to Defend the Right of Owners to Inscribed
Securities], *Рынок ценных бумаг* [The Securities Market], no. 13 (1997),
pp. 94-95; Kotov, note 43 above, pp. 73-74. Considering it to be the sole
obstacle in the path of vindication of paperless securities, Gorbikov and
Baranov even suggest it be eliminated by the introduction of a special
technology for recording paperless securities, which would enable each
of them "... also to trace the movement thereof from the first owner to the
last". It is doubtful that this is a way out of the situation, because it does
not answer all the other questions.

towards the transfer of property into ownership (in particular – purchase-sale and barter).

As a result the establishment and application of the concept of the *right of ownership to an incorporeal thing* has appeared, in particular – to a subjective civil right. Most dreadful is not the fact that not everyone understands the absurdity of the situation, but that the *overwhelming majority of practitioners (including judges) consider this to be normal, comprehensible in and of itself,* and the majority of scholars simply wave it aside.

To be sure, it is illustrative that the proponents of applying rights-to-a-thing means to the defense of rights comprising paperless securities are significantly fewer than proponents of extending to them the regime of right to a thing (which, it should be said, indirectly testifies also to the inconsistency of the position taken by them). Categorically "in favor" are only Korshunova[59] and Krylova;[60] and presumably in favour, Shatalov.[61] Categorically opposed to the *vindicatio* of paperless securities are not only we, not only all well-known representatives of academic science, but also the majority of practitioners,[62] and even – beginning scholars.[63]

---

[59] Korshunova, note 4 above, pp. 53-54.

[60] Krylova, note 4 above, p. 32.

[61] Shatalov, «Депонент и депозитарий: Вот тебе, бабушка, и Юрьев день» [Depositor and Depositary: Too Bad It Didn't Work], *Рынок ценных бумаг* [The Securities Market], no. 2 (1997), p. 65. In an article previously published, Shatalov took a much more correct position. See Shatalov, note 50 above, p. 67.

[62] See Gorbikov and Baranov, note 58 above, p. 94; Konovalov, note 42 above, p. 33; Kotov, note 43 above, pp. 73-74; Speranskii, note 6 above; Shatalov, note 50 above, p. 66.

[63] See, for example, S. Iu. Kann, *Защита прав владельцев ценных бумаг* [Defence or Rights of Possessors of Securities] (M., 2000), p. 8 (Dissertation abstract: канд. Юридических наук); Trofimenko, note 47 above; Iakovlev, note 11 above, pp. 11-12.

Naturally, the question is put – why did this happen? The reply can only be one – because that turned out to be more advantageous. It is obvious that even if one finds that specific individual who at one time was the first to suggest that a security be declared to be not a document, but a property right (or other "incorporeal thing"), even if one convinces him and compels him to make public repentance, all the same

(1) practice will not refrain from considering securities as the aggregate of subjective civil rights (with all the consequences arising therefrom);

(2) it remains incomprehensible how it happened that a subjective-right theory did not "find support in the person of individual representatives", but prevailed absolutely in practice, notwithstanding ceaseless criticism on the pages of the scholarly legal press.

Only one matter remains: *to declare securities to be the aggregate of rights* (or a corporeal thing, fiction, symbol – the essence does not change) and *from this point of view refer to practical activity that which has proved to be much more preferable than the traditional scholarly postulates*. It is a secret to no one that today both legislative norms and the postulates of legal science regard practice as a means of resolving determined tasks but not in order to justly resolve questions of rights and duties. It is no accident that in the pages of the press concepts of morality, justness, abuse, good faith, and reasonableness are being eroded: the more flexible they become, the better for practice! The fall in the prestige of the modern science of law also can not be considered to be accidental, in particular – the doctrines on legal norms and means of elucidating their meaning (or methods of interpretation). Today no one wants to ascertain the real meaning of a legal norm – this is of interest to no one. It is much more interesting to interpret a legal norm by knowing in advance what this interpretation must achieve.

In order to achieve such purposes, all means are good –

hence legislative provisions and "precedential decisions" are involved and, naturally, postulates of the science of law. Whereas in the Soviet period scholars frequently lamented that legal science weakly served the requirements of practice, today that cannot be said. Only this service has taken on a disfigured form that can only be imagined: science has turned out to be "running errands" for practice. If practice needs to create the institution of paperless securities – practice creates it; and you, learned scholars, prove its legality and substantiation. It is unimportant that it is illegal and unsubstantiated; this interests nobody. If "your science" does not enable the task to be achieved – we turn to another scholar. Naturally, his work will be well paid.

Having replied to the question why for legal practitioners it has proved to be more advantageous to reject the traditional documentary theory and to be guided by postulates of a speculative subjective-right conception of securities, we may ascertain the purpose whose achievement facilitates the latter conception. After this we must elicit the normal, classical means of achieving this purpose attended by a normal classical concept of a security and, having elicited these, be engaged with the question why other means having nothing in common with canonical civilistics should be preferred to such means.

Chapter 3: Paperless Securities and Securities from the
Position of a Philistine

IN ORDER to answer the questions put, it is necessary to answer
what securities represent in general and paperless securities,
in particular, *from the standpoint of practice* – not of a jurist,
but of an ordinary philistine, a dilettante in jurisprudence – an
economist, financier, manager, entrepreneur, banker, and so
on. Why is the viewpoint of a philistine of interest to us?
Because the legislative norms on which the subjective-right
concept of securities is built were written not by a jurist, but
by a philistine and have as their foundation that philistine
notion about the subject of regulation. There is nothing strange
in this, for the legislator is rather like a Kazakh or Kirgiz folk
poet, an *akyn*, who ascertains that which he observes and
relates that which, in his view, follows from this. The task of
the professional jurist – with the assistance of means of legal
hermeneutics is to give a *correct* – logically irreproachable,
reasonable, good-faith, just, and gracious – interpretation of
norms formulated by the legislator and then, with the assistance
of the means of the theory of law, draw from these norms
correct conclusions concerning the legal significance of the
factual circumstances of a specific case and the subjective rights
and legal duties arising from them.

And so, securities from the standpoint of a philistine, or
as is frequently said now, "of life", "according to concepts".
We turn from the law of ownership, incorporeal things,
vindicatio, possession, and other legal essences; we write as
we hear. And see.

From this position *documentary* securities differ little
from any other documents needed in order to effectuate the
rights certified by them. As we may have been convinced in
the course of our extensive practical activity, for the
nonprofessional it is all the same "what is Hamlet, what is

Winnie-the-Pooh", what is a stock, what is a contract, what is a laundry receipt: fail to present a stock – you are not admitted to a meeting; fail to show a contract, money is not forthcoming; fail to present a laundry receipt – you receive no laundry. In sum, a "documentary security" (document, paper) is regarded by the philistine as a *means necessary in order to achieve the principal purpose – the exisence and effectuation of a particular subjective right.* If there is the means – fine; if not – this is significantly worse, but not fatal, for even bearer securities may be reinstated (see Chapter 34, 2002 Code of Civil Procedure of the Russian Federation).

At some point the following question arises in the consciousness of the philistine: can one not resort to some *other means,* with whose assistance one might prove that you have a right and may, accordingly, receive something? For all of its convenience, the certification of rights with the assistance of a document in the hands of an empowered person is not without a number of shortcomings: the *empowered person must be concerned about the preservation of the document.* The document must not be lost. One must see that it is not burned, nor soaked, nor rotted, nor accidentally torn up by a favorite relative. One must take measures so that the document is not stolen nor forged, that the representative has not sold it by abuse of trust, and so on.[64] If, God forbid, something similar occurs, the individual is confronted with or undergoes visits to bureaucrats, directors, courts, laws, and other torments, or

---

[64] To this list may be added a reference to a number of other circumstances which in Russian conditions are transformed into problems. It is more complex and disadvantageous to keep documents, the more valuable and numerous they are. Documents may always be sealed, described, and arrested (or seized); for example, as material evidence in a criminal case – judged then by the Ministry of Internal Affairs or the Procuracy! Finally, in the process of concluding transactions it is essential to be concerned about the correctness of formalizing the transfer thereof, and with respect to order and inscribed securities – also compliance with the requirements for formalizing inscriptions on the documents themselves.

simply reconciles himself to the loss of rights which has occurred, the former not necessarily excluding the last.

Demand creates a proposal. From the requirements enumerated grows a means of certifying rights without virtually any of the said shortcomings – *the official fixation (or entry) of rights*; that is, the consolidation of such "in a special register (ordinary or computer)" (Article 142(2), Civil Code), "by a person who has received a special license ... including in paperless form (with the assistance of means of computer technology, and so on)" (Article 149(1), Civil Code). An empowered person need no longer be concerned with the preservation of the document – he simply does not have it. The "person having a special license" is concerned about everything – he acts so that the official fixation (or entry) effectuated by him corresponds to reality, so that it, God forbid, is not distorted, are not erased, are not lost. He also "... is obliged upon the demand of the possessor of the right to issue a document to him testifying to the consolidated right" (Article 149(1), Civil Code); that is, to confirm, when necessary, that yes, in fact, such and such rights do indeed belong to such and such a person. Accordingly, the granting, transfer, or limitation of rights being so fixed must be reflected in the entries of the person effectuating the official fixation (Article 149(2), Civil Code).

An empowered person thus no longer carries risks connected with the material nature of the document: he simply has no such document and will not so long as he himself does not wish to. A third person is concerned about everything, officially effectuating the fixation of rights. It is sufficient for an empowered person to know that the licensed "third person"
(1) opened in his, the empowered person's, name a deposit account or personal account in the register;
(2) wrote down that in the respective account were "entered" a particular quantity of such "securities".

To be sure, no one ever saw these securities (they are paperless), but this is unimportant because the principal value for the empowered person is not the "securities" themselves, "entered in the account", but the circumstance that *with the fact of a determined quantity of securities being in an account as documents concerning the issue and registration of the issue of these securities is connected recognition for the empowered persons of determined subjective rights* which correspond to respective legal duties of the person who issued these "securities".

Immediately there emerge several (at a minimum, four) "buts".

First. Yes, the *empowered person* no longer has a document. *But!* This does not mean there is no document at all. The entry of information concerning subjective rights having an official character is something, strictly speaking, that is called a document and remains such.[65] But with a third person. In reality this means *the risks connected with the documentary nature of the means of fixation of subjective rights do not disappear, but are merely otherwise distributed* (in the classical

---

[65] In this sense the name of the form of fixation of subject rights with the assistance of computer technology as "paperless" is, of course, imprecise. At the same time, this observation does not impart an expansive interpretation and extend it also to the term "paperless securities". See, for example, A. Gabov and P. Iani, «Арест ценных бумаг по уголовному делу» [Arrest of Securities in a Criminal Case], *Российская юстиция* [Russian Justice], no. 8 (1999). Used text contained in Data Base Garant Maksimum; K. Okunev, [Phenomenon of Paperless Security], Кодекс-INFO: Информационный бюллетень текущего законодательства [Kodeks-INFO: Information Bulletin of Current Legislation], no. 18 (1998); used text in Data Base Kodeks. It is wholly adequate, "securities" have no documentary form of embodiment, they are truly paperless, existing only as an image. Gabov and Iani deny even the term "paperless security" as supposedly absent in legislation, which, first, is simply not true and, second, in and of itself can not serve as a reason for rejecting its use by legal science.

security the empowered person bears them, and in the case of paperless – they fall in a third person).

Second. Insofar as the risks of loss, destruction, damage, distortion, stealing, and forgery of documents, and the great majority of other risks are preserved also in the case of the "paperless form of fixation", an essential condition for the practical application of this institution is the interest of the person effectuating the fixation in the minimization of these risks, reducing them to zero. *But*! This does not happen. The principle of reasonableness predetermines the postulate that *he to whom a right belongs, that is, the empowered person, should be concerned for the preservation of the right, means of certification thereof, proof, and effectuation*. He is the most interested that nothing happen to the document certifying his right which might diminish that right. The institution of paperless fixation presupposes that *rights belonging to the third person with respect to the subject effectuating the fixation are being fixed*. There are no decisive grounds to suppose that a person who is a stranger to the empowered person will be concerned for the protection of rights better than the empowered person himself. In this event, when the fixation is effectuated by a person obliged to the respective bearer of the rights (or emittent of the securities), weighty grounds appear to suppose the reverse, that the person effectuating the official entry of rights will by fair means or foul endeavor to protect, first, his own and the emittent's interests. Must one be reminded that the interests of the obliged person exclude the interests of the empowered person?

Third. As already noted, we do not dispute the possibility of the existence of documents on an electronic carrier and welcome the progressive development of means of an electronic entry of information and the arising on the basis thereof of new forms of certifying subjective civil rights, including those which until recently were usually certified by emission securities.[66] *But*! One cannot fail to be aware that the use of any new technologies for the fixation of subject rights must have as a condition the existence of means enabling risks caused exclusively the use of these new technologies to be minimized. It is no secret to anyone that *at present there still do not exist technologies for systems of defense of computer information that can not be broken.* Instances of unsanctioned penetration into computer networks for the purpose of destroying and distorting information can not be prevented by such mighty organizations as the United States Department of Defense, the Savings Bank of the Russian Federation, and the Bank of New York. They already have been led and are leading to weekly stealing of monetary means whose amounts are calculated in millions of dollars. Accordingly, the more that computer technologies for the fixation of rights comprising paperless securities are used, the greater the risks of the persons empowered with regard to them to be deprived of such or to receive them in unrecognizable form.

Fourth. Criminalistics technologies for the discovery of forgery and distortion of information fixed on a paper bearer, technologies for the establishment of the initial content thereof and search for a person who effectuated an unsanctioned change of a paper document have been worked on for centuries. Accordingly, even if "someone, somewhere, now and then" began to steal, for example, order securities and to forge the name of the legal holder specified thereon, sooner or later this fact inevitably will be discovered, and the person, in the course of time, certainly be found. *But*! *Analogous technologies enabling one to ascertain who distorted information, and when, fixed on a network server, what was the initial content thereof, and who distorted such, do not exist at present.* Naturally, nothing prevents paper documentation to be raised – files of transfer instructions, certificates concerning the right to an

---

66 See our abstract, note 13 above, pp. 8, 20-26; Belov, «Юридическая природа ...», note 13 above, p. 23; and others.

inheritance, execution, and other analogous documents, on the basis of which electronic entries are formed. In this event it should be acknowledged that the fixation of rights in reality is effectuated not in electronic, but in paper, form.

Iarotskii, not fascinated by the various criminalistics aspects of the problem, confined himself merely to mentioning the simple, everyday aspects characteristic for the level of development of computer technologies in modern Russia:

> The possessor of a paperless security also will risk losing the possibility of effectuating the rights expressed therein. This, for example, may occur as a result of a failure in the work of the computer where respective information is kept in the absence of a back-up in other information bearers also the possibility of the possessor thereof to prove his rights based on a paperless security by means of presenting an extract from the register. A risk of this nature may be reduced only by recording the information concerning the possessors of paperless securities on several independent information carriers independent of one another.[67]

What, thus, is received "in life"? What does the philistine see in paperless securities? He sees the following:
(1) he entrusts the fixation of his rights to a person who is much less interested in this than he himself, or even is not interested at all;
(2) the risks which the person fixing the rights places on himself are not only somewhat not lower, but even higher than those which the empowered person himself bears who is concerned about the preservation of the document in his hands;

---

[67] V. Iarotskii, "Риск в правоотношениях по ценным бумагам" [Risk in Legal Relations With Regard to Securities], *Российская юстиция* [Russian Justice], no. 7 (2000); we used the text in Data Base "Garant-Maksimum".

(3) a number of risks falling on the person effectuating the fixation of rights existing technology does not allow to be avoided at all.[68]

In light of all that has been said, no one is guaranteed that having once turned to the person effectuating the fixation of rights with a demand to confirm the fixed rights, or to make changes in existing entries concerning the rights, he is received and learns with surprise that he, it turns out, six months ago sold his securities to company "X", is no longer entered in the register, and, accordingly, *has no rights*. Of course, our philistine has sold nothing. Someone simply brought an instruction of transfer, supposedly signed by an "empowered representative of the registered person" concerning the "withdrawal" of the paperless securities from his account and the entry thereof in the account of company "X", and the registrar fulfilled this instruction. Or someone (most often, of course, the registrar himself) for mercenary purposes autonomously "threw over" the securities to the account of the person who controls him, of course, having in advance concocted the notorious "instructions of transfer" with forged signatures of the registered persons.

---

[68] One of the most objective of our opponents shares the view that "the Certificate most reliably defends the rights of possessors of a security". See Lysikhin, «Удостоверение и реализация прав по эмиссионным ценным бумагам» [Certification and Realization of Rights With Regard to Emission Securities], *Рынок ценных бумаг* [The Securities Market], no. 18 (1996), p. 64. He goes on (p. 65) to elicit the risks inherent in the paperless form of fixing rights, including – the accurate name thereof being "the problem of independence of the possessor from the unfairness of the register holder".

Chapter 4: What is Violated? Or the Basic Question of the Theory of Paperless Securities

---

WE NOW look at the situation through the eyes of a jurist. Insofar as the text below is directed only to specialists, that is, to persons having respective training and qualifications, we commence directly with the main issue, not being afraid that we will not be understood. Jurists must understand.

The division of subjective civil rights into *absolute* and *relative* is well-known. Given a certain indefiniteness of the criteria for such division and a discussion concerning the existence and essence of a third category of rights (mixed, absolute-relative), one may consider it to be established that the bearer of an absolute right is counterbalanced by each and every person as an obliged person, distinct from an empowered person, and the possessor of a relative right is one specific individually-determined person (also not coinciding with an empowered person).

Thus, an owner to whom the right of ownership ensures the possibility to perform any actions with a thing which is the object thereof is counterbalanced by all other persons obliged to refrain from an infringement of the right of ownership itself, the object thereof, and the process of effectuation. The right of ownership is thus a typical absolute right. On the contrary, the right of a purchaser to demand the transfer of a thing to him corresponds to the duty of one specific person (the seller) to transfer the respective thing. No one other than the seller is obliged to transfer the thing to the purchaser. Consequently, the right of obligation (demand) is a classical relative right.

From the foregoing explanation it is evident that rights comprising the content of securities, including paperless, may by their nature only be *relative rights*. The possessor of such rights is the subject registered in this capacity by the person officially effectuating the fixation of rights, that is, as legislation in force says, the "registered person". The bearer of duties corresponding to the said rights will be the emittent of the paperless securities.

Suppose the empowered person with regard to paperless stocks is the person registered in the stockholder register as a stockholder ("possessor of securities"). He has the right to be admitted to participate in a general meeting of stockholders, and in certain instances – the right to demand the convocation thereof, take part in the discussion and adoption of decisions with regard to questions on the agenda of the meeting, demand consideration of the question concerning the payment of dividends, payment of declared dividends, and certain other rights. The joint-stock society – the emittent of the respective stocks – is the person on whom depends the effectuation of these rights, the person who is obliged to admit the stockholder to the meeting, convoke the meeting, be guided by decisions adopted by the meeting, consider the question concerning the payment of a dividend. pay declared dividends, and so on.

There is no more immutable truth in legal science than that *a violation of a subjective right may ensue only on the part of the bearer of the duty corresponding to this subjective right*. Accordingly, an absolute right may be violated by each and every, and a relative right – only by one, individually-determined, specific person.

Any person may steal a thing, damage it, obstruct the owner in possessing the thing or in using it, and so on. Accordingly, any person who has violated an absolute right comes to be in a new relative legal relation with the victim – a delictual (tort) legal relation (for compensation of harm) or *condictio* legal relation (unsubstantiated enrichment). At the same time, only that person to whom a demand has been addressed, that is the seller, may violate the right of demand of the purchaser concerning the transfer of a thing. Only the seller may refuse to transfer the thing, transfer a poor-quality thing, delay transfer of the thing, deliver it to another place than that in which it was subject to delivery according to the arrangement, and so on. All those same actions performed by a third person (who is not the seller) do not constitute violations of the rights of the purchaser.

Certain doubts arise when the violation of a relative right has as its cause the actions of third persons. But upon closer examination it is determined that in this instance the principle that "only he who is obliged to someone may be the violator of a right" remains immutable. We consider the following example. Say that a seller who is driving his own motor vehicle to a purchaser in order to receive a monetary amount due to him under a contract of purchase-sale has an accident, the driver of the other means of transport being at fault. As a result, the seller is forced to discontinue the trip to the purchase, returns home, restores his health, repairs the motor vehicle, rings the purchaser, agrees on the time and place of a new meeting, and only then (that is, a rather material delay) receives the money. May he demand from the purchaser the payment of interest for the delay? Obviously, not: the purchaser violated nothing and had the seller been on time – he would have paid within the period. This means the seller has the right to receive the interest from the person at fault in the road transport accident as ... as what? Only as compensation for losses caused by the violation of a property interest, but not as the demand (right of obligation) of a seller.

Now we turn to the instance described at the end of the preceding paragraph when a person effectuating the fixation of rights comprising paperless securities – depository or registrar – inserted changes in an entry concerning rights (say, of a stockholder) not sanctioned by an empowered person. What has happened? A person previously empowered has ceased to be such, lost the rights belonging to him without an expression of will for such. As a result, he has not proved his status as a stockholder, did not attend a meeting, did not receive dividends, and so on. It is beyond doubt that something here has been violated, but what? *What subjective civil right is violated and by whom is it violated when making changes in the register of possessors of securities which diminish, limit, or deprive the possessor of paperless securities belonging to him?* – this is the question which has become the stumbling-block of practice and by a strange confluence of circumstances avoided scholarly attention. By analogy with the term "basic question of philosophy", this problem might be designated as the "basic question of the theory of paperless securities".

Before beginning to seek an answer to it, one must make several reservations. First. Any reply to the question put will be accepted favorably by legal practice only in the event of compliance with the following condition: the *reply must not in any event exclude the possibility of restoring the former possessor of the securities in the rights belonging to him.* It is similar to an owner of a unique stolen thing being interested only in its return, and not in receiving monetary compensation, just as a stockholder is interested not in contributory compensation for losses but in the return to him of the rights of a stockholder. Whereas usually monetary contributory compensation satisfies the owner of stolen things, and interest in demanding and obtaining that stolen in kind is rather the exception than the rule, the former stockholder, on the contrary, wishes namely to acquire his status as a stockholder and compensation in money is not very attractive to him.

Moreover, in a number of instances a stockholder is interested not only in the return to him of paperless securities (rights) of which he was deprived without substantiation, but also in *imparting retroactive force to the return of the paperless securities*; that is, making official entries such that the paperless securities belonged to him always and never left him. This phenomenon in practice is designated by the term "restoration of entry in a register" (in the deposit account), which, of course, does not reflect the essence of the concept concealed by it, but there are less grounds to replace it with any other. The retroactive force of restored entries is necessary to the stockholders who have suffered to have the opportunity to contest all decisions of stockholder meetings adopted with the participation of the other person.[69]

The second reservation, or more precisely, the second requirement to which a reply to the basic question formulated above must correspond, — will be these. The reply *must preserve the possibility of the presentation by the person who suffered of demands against the so-called "real defendants"*, that is, above all and depending on the situation – against the emittent of the securities, depository, and registrar, and the persons from which, in the extreme event one does not succeed in restoring in rights, one may receive something.

The least viable is the reply, which supposes the possibility of bringing merely a suit concerning losses against the natural person who changed the content of the data base or committed the forgery of the signature of the instruction of transfer. The search for them is, as a rule, not successful, and in those rare instances in which one succeeds in discovering them, simply nothing proves to be received from them.[70] Such

---

[69] In imparting retroactive force to an act of restoration of entries the possessors of securities are interested also because this enables all transactions concluded with them to be contested – to demand and obtain from the debtor all payments following with regard to securities for the period during which the entries were restored. For these purposes stockholders are not alone: possessors of State paperless securities and corporative bonds (bondholders) pursue identical purposes also when demanding their "restoration in rights".

[70] In our day we too proposed this way of resolving the problem, true, together with another – a suit for losses against the registrar. See Belov, *Защита интересов* ..., note 13 above, pp. 38-39. Also see: Gorbinkov and Baranov, note 13 above, p. 94; and on the following page, our commentary on this publication; Konovalov, note 42 above, p. 33. Recovery of losses from the registrar also is favored by Iuldashbaeva, note 12 above, p. 93.

measures of defense proposed in the academic literature (we observe – as dissertation theses) of rights of victims as possessors of paperless securities, which include the recovery of a legal penalty and compensation of losses in the amount of the difference "... between the amount paid for the security and the value of the security at the moment of filing suit or the price for which such security was sold on the market ...",[71] testify to a complete unfamiliarity of the author of those proposals with the requirements and interests of modern investors, and in the eyes of the last appear to be simple mockery.

The stockholders who have suffered will not be content with replies that a violation of their rights has occurred arising from a contract with the depositary or from the prescriptions of a law (if one refers to relations with the registrar). Why? Because even having proved that the depositary effectuated the withdrawal of paperless securities from a deposit account in violation of the provision of the depositary contract, and the registrar —in violation of the Rules for keeping the register established by he himself and publicly disclosed, the victim can never obtain from them restoration in rights. Again, why? Is it so difficult for the depositary and registrar to annul the entries made without substantiation and restore the previous ones? Yes, it is difficult, we would even say, impossible since by their actions the depositary and registrar deprive another person of paperless securities, at whose expense the victim will be restored in rights. A new problem arises: on what grounds? If we succeed in proving the lack of good faith of the new possessor it will be good, but what if not? How to explain to the new possessor of paperless securities that the instruction concerning the entry thereof in his account is invalid, being signed by an unempowered person of the predecessor?

And, finally, a third reservation. In discussing what has been violated and by whom, we unavoidably will touch upon

---

71 Kann, note 63 above, pp. 8, 9.

questions of the legal status of not only the emittent of
securities and holders thereof, but also third persons with
respect to each of them – the *depositary* and the *registrar*.
Figures with analogous names, just as the institute of paperless
securities itself, are not a Russian invention and exist both in
Western Europe and in the United States. It is regrettable only
that the *similarity of names does not go farther*. An emittent is
obliged to issue a normal classical security, a document, to
any empowered person who so wishes, even in the event of
the "paperless" form itself, "at their place". "There" the
possibility to demand the issue of a security (or "security
certificate" – according to the terminology of modern
legislation and practice) belongs to investors only if the issue
of securities in documentary form has been provided for.

"There" depositaries work only on a market of normal,
classical securities – documents which they keep and manage;
legal relations arising in so doing are formalized (once again,
at the wish of the client) by the issue of a so-called *deposit
certificate* – a document certifying the acceptance for keeping
of a determined number of securities and having the status of
a security.[72] In Russia depositaries act as an intermediate link
between the registrars and investors, replace registrars,
"nominally hold" paperless securities belonging to investors,
which is certified by a depositary contract and periodically
issued extracts from the deposit account suitable only for
placing in toilets.

"There" the registrars not merely register something in
a register (rights, symbols, fictions, aggregates, and so on),
but also certify legal relations in which they become with

---

[72] Proposals concerning the introduction of such a document in Russia
under the name of a "warehouse certificate" were made by us in 1996.
See Belov, *Ценные бумаги ...*, note 13 above, pp. 143-144, 401, but
remained unnoticed. Naturally the book was written by "some
postgraduate at a law faculty" and not an employee of the Federal
Securities Commission or the Bank of Russia.

respect to investors the issuers of documents having the status of securities – *securities certificates*.[73] In Russia we do not speak of such certificates; registrars at best "register" facts of contributing money for something which no one has ever seen, and then – facts of alienation and acquisition of this "incomprehensible something". Not a single paper remains in the hands of the investor formalizing his legal relations with the registrar.

We do not have at all registrars in the Western sense of the word. And the same with regard to certificates. We "forgot" about them during the heat of privatization. In their place is a series of extracts from the register ... This is like issuing a passport without the signature and seal of the police division or birth certificate without the signature and seal of the section of the Registry of Acts of Civil Status".[74]

Analogous thoughts but with respect to Russian depositaries have been expressed by another, although less well-known stock market professional, Esaulkova. Considering the concept recently foisted on us of American depositary receipts (ADRs), she wrote: "In essence ADRs are derivative securities ... certifying the right of ownership[75] of their possessor to part of the stocks in one of the foreign companies and giving the right to receive dividends, and also to part of the assets of the enterprise in the event of its liquidation.[76] From the legal point of view a depositary receipt is a certificate

---

[73] At one time similar documents – stock certificates – existed in Russia. See points 54-58, Statute on Joint-Stock Societies, 23 December 1990, No. 601. *СП РСФСР* (1991), no. 6, item 92. See note 38 above. Under the name "surrogate certificate" we proposed to retain and use them not only for stocks, but for any other securities. Belov, note 72 above, pp. 142-143, 401.

[74] B. Alekhin, "Метаморфозы трансфер-агента и регистратора" [Metamorphoses of Transfer-Agent and Registrar], *Рынок ценных бумаг* [The Securities Market], no. 17 (1996), p. 36.

[75] Imprecise. Of course the reference should be to a right of demand.

[76] That is, the property rights of the stockholder.

concerning the deposit of stocks in the amount of a depositary bank – the emittent of the ADR".[77] Shatalov expressed it analogously and somewhat more precisely: "… the rights of a client of a nominee holder [paperless securities – *V. B.*] are merely rights of demand [for the provision of paperless securities – *V. B.*] against the nominee holder".[78]

Having in view the reservations made, we shall endeavour to reply to the question as to which right is violated and by whom as a result of the unsubstantiated change of entries with regard to a deposit account or personal account in the register of possessors of paperless securities. Obviously, only one of two answers is possible: (a) the *rights* themselves *comprising paperless securities* are violated, and (b) some absolute *right to paperless securities* is violated. We shall consider each of the variants.

---

[77] T. Esaulkova, "Конвертация акций российских эмитентов в АДР" [Conversion of Stocks of Russian Emittents into ADRs", *Рынок ценных бумаг* [The Securities Market], no. 9 (1998), p. 8.
[78] Shatalov, note 61 above, p. 65.

Chapter 5: Suppose That Rights Comprising Paperless Securities Were Violated

---

MOST ATTRACTIVE, of course, is the answer that a violation occurred of *rights comprising paperless securities*. Thus, if stocks were withdrawn from the account of a person in the register without substantiation, this means that the *rights of a stockholder* were violated and, accordingly, the stockholder has the right to have recourse for the defense thereof. Russian judicial practice takes this position, although one can not fail to acknowledge that it is rather inconsistent. We endeavor to take this view to the end without being constrained by existing practice.

   The relative nature of the rights of a stockholder presuppose that they may be violated only by the joint-stock society itself – the emittent of the stocks. The person who has suffered should present all demands to it, to the emittent of the stocks, in particular – concerning recognition of the rights of the stockholder and restoration thereof. From this, and only from this, should one proceed when deciding the question of the rights of a stockholder who has suffered.

   The actions of the emittent who has received such demands will depend upon the situation. (1) **The emittent itself is engaged in recording the affiliation of paperless securities.** In this situation the emittent is obliged with regard to establishing the substantiation of the demand presented to recognize the right of the stockholder, to annul entries illegally made, and restore the old ones. After the restoration is made, the entire gravity of the problem falls on the emittent, who for a certain period will be in a state of expectation of claims on the part of the person for whose account the former stockholder was restored in rights. Upon the receipt of such claims, and then suits, the emittent should demand evidence from the plaintiff of the substantiation of receipt in his account of the disputed stocks and upon the submission by it of such evidence (for example, an instruction of transfer with a forged or unempowered signature) – discredit it.

(2) *Paperless stocks have been recorded at a special registrar – that is, a person with whom the emittent is in contractual relations*. In this event the emittent itself may restore the victim in the rights lost by him only *factually*, that is, simply note in its entries that in fact the stocks belong not to who is named in the register, but to the victim. He must be admitted to stockholder meetings, dividends paid to him, and so on. But *legally* the restoration does not happen because in the entries of the registrar the rights of stockholder are entered for another person, and this deprives the stockholder who suffered of the possibility to dispose of the stocks and preserves for the illegal acquirer the legal basis to demand from the emittent the performance of its duties to him. So that *legal restoration* has occurred the emittent or victim stockholder should apply to the registrar with a demand of analogous content. But the emittent is deprived of the possibility to declare such a demand since the stockholder went to the emittent with a demand to eliminate the violation of the *rights of a stockholder*, and the emittent, by virtue of not having the rights of a stockholder, can not meet such a demand. The victim stockholder itself also can not demand from the registrar the elimination of the violation of the rights of a stockholder since the registrar does not bear duties corresponding thereto and in principle can not violate these rights.

Nor can the emittent proceed with an autonomous suit against the registrar based on the fact of recognition of the demands of the stockholder who suffered. It would be pleasant to believe that, although this does not follow from the legislation, the existence of a specialist registrar for the rights of stockholders deprives of any legal force an entry of the emittent itself concerning its own stockholders. An emittent which declares to a registrar that it recognizes as a stockholder not who has been entered in the register, but his predecessor, will seem rather pale. The registrar will reply to the emittent something in the nature of that this is your problem: you may recognize as a stockholder whomsoever you wish, but I have registered in the register all those who are – please be so kind as to perform your duties.

There remain the sole grounds for an autonomous suit of the emittent against the registrar – violation by the last of the provisions of the contract for keeping the register. But satisfaction of such a suit also is problematic since one can not always establish a violation of that contract. Practice shows that questions concerning documents are grounds for making entries in the register, the formalization thereof, and the procedure for submission usually are not affected in contracts between an emittent and registrar, and therefore the registrar has violated nothing.

(3) *Paperless stocks were lost at the depositary – person with whom the person who suffered is in contractual relations but the emittent has no such relations.* Possibly the victim will have the right to demand the restoration of entries directly from the depositary, referring to norms of the depositary contract and the absence of grounds for withdrawal of stocks for the account of the person to whom the stocks were credited. But such a demand has no relation to the violation of the *rights of a stockholder* and can not have as its result the restoration thereof.

A constructing a chain analogous to that considered above (stockholder – emittent – depositary), we again encounter the impossibility of the effectuation by the emittent of a genuine "legal" restoration of the victim in the rights of a stockholder. The "actual restoration" effectuated will not be binding either on the depositary or on third persons, including he in whose deposit account the disputed stocks proved to be. But even if such restoration were deemed to be binding upon the person who received the stocks in his deposit account without substantiation, all the same the emittent will not have grounds to force the depositary to annul the entries made by it and to perform the restoration. A completely inexplicable situation has formed: entries in the deposit account will not reflect the real state of affairs, which will be established from the materials of the case with regard to defense of the rights of a stockholder between the emittent and victim, with the participation of the new acquirer of the stocks.[79]

The fact that all attempts to be guided by one of the three approaches considered above leads to a logical legal dead end, and that none of the aforesaid attempts is used in practice eloquently testifies to the incorrectness of our suggestion, proceeding from which this entire chapter has been written. It is not paradoxical, but the *unsubstantiated withdrawal of paperless securities by a registrar from a personal account or by a depositary from a deposit account does not entail a violation of rights comprising paperless securities*, including when the emittent itself is the registrar.

The classification of rights violated by the unsubstantiated withdrawal of paperless securities as rights comprising the content of these very paperless securities also has other shortcomings.

Thus, the demands of a stockholder against the emittent and of the emittent against the registrar and depositary concerning the restoration of the person who suffered in the rights of stockholder prove to be in principle not fulfillable in a situation when at the moment of presentation of this demand the quantity of stocks in the account in which at one time the disputed stocks were credited turn out to be insufficient. In other words, the construction only works in a situation when the disputed stocks have not yet been withdrawn from the account of the first acquirer immediately after the victim. The situation becomes simple hopeless if the personal (or deposit)

---

[79] On an analogous situation, but construed otherwise, see Shatalov, note 61 above, pp. 64-65.

account of the person who directly acquired the disputes stocks at the moment of presentation of the demand concerning restoration of rights proves to be closed. In this event the restoration proves to be impossible since the person who may be defeated in stockholder rights to the benefit of the victim simply does not exist.

The situation is more confusing if the person who suffered or the emittent involved by him in the proceeding can not prove the bad faith of the person into whose account the disputed stocks "went" from the account of the person who suffered. It is one matter when this occurred under an instruction of transfer with a forged signature, and the forgery was organized or committed by the person into whose account the stocks were transferred. But what if the first acquirer of the stocks acted in good faith? This may happen, say, when he concluded a transaction of purchase-sale with the person who presented himself as the representative of the stockholder. To accuse an acquirer that he did not recognize a forged power of attorney can not be done. It should not be forgotten that the forgery may not be recognized by someone else – the registrar or depositary, who compare a signature on a power of attorney with a sample available on the questionnaire of the registered person or card with sample signatures. If someone is to be accused – namely them, how is the acquirer not in good faith.

Thus, the construction is built on the base of the most obvious and reasonable version – unsubstantiated withdrawal of paperless securities entails a violation of rights comprising these paperless securities – proves to be defective. It is workable only in the most simple situation – when there is a coincidence of identity of the registrar with the identity of the emittent, the presence in the personal account immediately after the acquirer who suffered of a quantity of securities sufficient for the restoration in rights, and the lack of good faith of such. Other must more common and regrettable situations it is not capable of resolving. nor even of simply explaining, and therefore the proposal being examined must be abandoned as incorrect. In essence, practice already has abandoned it as having no prospects.

Although the phrase "defense of rights of a stockholder" continues to have a stamp of approval in scholarly works and judicial acts, and in the practice of so-called business advocates, in fact that being defended by courts is something else – *absolute rights to paperless securities*. Consequently, according to the logic of things, should they also be deemed to be violated?

Chapter 6: Suppose That Rights in Paperless Securities Were Violated

AND SO we come to an analysis of the second proposition, which consists of the following. Paperless securities, undoubtedly, represent a certain property value, and that *must be a certain property right formalizing the affiliation of this value to a determined person and the alienability of such against all third persons*, and thus a *specific absolute right*. The fact that paperless securities represent relative subjective civil rights (for example, the very rights of a stockholder) and, accordingly, the introduction into turnover of the category of an "absolute right to a relative right" is not uncontroversial – from this we abstract and will not take this into account. We clarify that this value shall remain for the moment "in brackets", which we shall open a bit later below.

Thus, a property value. The person who as a result of another's illegal actions (emittent, or registrar, or depositary, or someone else – this is not an issue of principle) has lost this property value, experienced a diminution of his absolute property right, must be deemed the *person to whom property harm (or damage) has been caused*. In accordance with Article 1064(1) of the Civil Code, "Harm caused ... to the property of a citizen, and also harm caused to the property of a juridical person, shall be subject to compensation in full by the person who caused the harm". Points (2) and (3) of this Article clarify that the duty to compensate harm caused arises, according to the general rule, only in the event of it being caused by *guilty* and *illegal* (or unlawful) actions. Consequently, the person who someone by his illegal and guilty actions has deprived of paperless stocks belonging to him must be deemed, first, a *victim of the diminution of his property sphere* and, second, *to have acquired a right of demand for compensation of harm caused.*

The Civil Code (Article 1082) knows two means of compensation for property harm. The first – *compensation of harm in kind* – is reflected in the provision to the victim of a thing (or property) of the same kind and quality, rectification of a damaged thing, or other similar actions. The second means – *compensation of losses* – is monetary compensation of the value of the lost property, expenses for the restoration thereof, and also lost advantage.

Compensation of losses is legally possible always and for everything. So long as money is not abolished, so long the concept of a universal equivalent and legal tender is not abolished, compensation of losses will be the universal civil-law means of defense for any violated property interests. Has not the dawn begun to appear for resolving the problem? This is not the case, since *monetary compensation does not return to the victim stockholder the main thing – his stockholder rights*, that is, the major requirement presented by practitioners for an answer to the basic question of the theory of paperless securities is not met. We remind ourselves of the second requirement of practice for an answer to the Main Question – to ensure the possibility of presenting a suit against a real, solvent defendant – we with sorrow are forced to state that we receive the *least viable reply*.[80]

Having in view the shortcomings noted of compensation of losses, logically one should turn to investigating the question of the applicable of compensation of harm cause in kind. To do this, we must open the "brackets" – establish what is concealed by the conditional designation we have adopted, "property value", learn *precisely what* has been diminished, *what does the celebrated "in kind" consist of, and what lies*

---

[80] One advocate with whom we have had the honour to set out this position called it the "position of swindlers". In a certain sense he is right, but it should not be forgotten that this is the sole position that rests entirely on legislation. Does not this fact produce the most distressing reflections?

ahead in compensating the harm caused. The answer is rather depressing – in *subjective civil rights of a relative orientation that do not always have a property character.* The right of participation in the management of a joint-stock society, thanks to the restoration of which everything is organized, is of a nonproperty character.

But the property and nonproperty character of subjective rights of which the victim was arbitrarily deprived – this is not a disaster. Much worse is the legal mess into which we have fallen. Only the *emittent of paperless securities* may restore in relative rights; that is, the person who granted these rights, the person who is the bearer of duties corresponding to them, or (at least) – public authority. But to have recourse with a demand concerning compensation of harm in kind against the emittent is *illegal* generally since it is not obligatory that the deprivation of paperless securities occurred by reason of the commission of illegal guilty actions by the emittent itself.

To have recourse with a similar demand against the person at fault for causing the harm is *inconceivable.* It is good if this is the emittent. But if it is an employee of the depositary or registrar who maliciously transfers the stocks to the account of a "sham" company founded by him? How may a natural person restore someone in stockholder rights? How may a juridical person which is not the emittent of the stocks groundlessly withdrawn from an account do this? It can not be done; obviously this is objectively impossible, and it is impossible to oblige the performance thereof.

The piquancy of the situation is that *although no one except the emittent of paperless securities may restore them* (since, and this we constantly bear in mind, paperless securities are relative subjective civil rights), *whosoever finds it advantageous may deprive a registered person of paperless securities* (relative rights). It is not at all obligatory that this was the emittent. A person who by means of swindling achieved the transfer of another's paperless securities deprives another of relative rights belonging to him; however, to return the situation to the previous position he is not in a state to do since he does not grant such relative rights and objectively can not do so. The exception comprises an instance when the person by means of swindling transfers paperless securities *to his own name*, or (irrespective of stealing securities) is the holder of other paperless securities of the same kind and quality. If at the moment of consideration of the case there is a sufficient quantity of such in his account, then we think of a *suit concerning the recovery of a determined number of paperless securities* – that very number of which the former possessor was illegally deprived.

Thus, the duty with regard to compensation of harm caused in kind proves to be performable only in that situation when in the account of the causer of harm there is that quantity of paperless securities which equal or exceed that quantity which as a result of the unlawful guilty actions the victim was deprived. Demands concerning compensation of harm addressed to third persons (persons in whose accounts the disputed paperless securities subsequently fell) turn out to be unsubstantiated and are not subject to satisfaction since these persons have not caused any harm to the victim.[81]

---

[81] Except, of course, it is difficult to prove an instance when they acted in collusion with the direct causer of harm; that is, have the status of co-causers.

Chapter 7: Absolute Right to the Ideal "Something"

TO DATE "property value" conceals relative subjective civil rights, and indeed not always property, and even such a universal construction as compensation of harm caused in kind does not serve the cause of defending them. This circumstance leads to one important conclusion and explains much.

The *conclusion* is simple, but not obvious to everyone without the discussion we have had above. If we continue once and for all to open the parentheses and expose the relative subjective civil rights – that is, all there is to know about paperless securities – if we do not close the "brackets" forever, having recognized *these "brackets" themselves* to be the paperless securities, and not that which is confined within them (not relative property rights), then we have, when searching for means of defense of the said violated rights, to pass up the opportunity as an axiom concerning the possibility of a violation of relative rights only by the obliged subject. Otherwise, that is, recalling that which was concealed in "brackets", it follows that one should renounce completely efforts to fine a universal means of such defense because *classical civilistics does not know means of defense of relative rights against violations on the part of persons outside the relative legal relation.* The second answer satisfies neither science nor practice, and this means it is to be discarded.

This means it is essential to "close the brackets" and declare that *paperless securities are an ideal essence, with the existence of a notion concerning which is linked the notion concerning relative subjective civil rights comprising that value thanks to which the essence itself is thought of,* such as a distinctive "something". To be sure, such a "definition" should trouble any attentive reader because it does not correspond to any legal definition – not to the definition of the Civil Code, according to which securities are documents and paperless securities are property rights – nor to the approach of the Federal Law on Securities, according to which all securities, including paperless, are property rights. No place is left for a "peculiar something" in any act. We will keep this inconsistency "in mind" without delving into the reasons and significance thereof.

As regards the *explanation* promised above, the subject thereof is the aforesaid modern practical situation in accordance with which paperless securities – the "something" – are thought of as objects of an absolute right – a right protected against and every violation, even when the object thereof is with a third person who has not violated this right. The right, it turns out, consequently, is fuller, more exclusive, and independent for no one except a "registered person". What absolute right most fully meets the aforementioned characteristics? You do not need to be a genius to reply: of course, the *right of ownership*.

Can an incorporeal something be an object of the right of ownership? Above we answered that question in the negative. It also was said that if we come to the conclusion that paperless securities are something incorporeal, ideal, but not identical with subjective rights, this means it is *necessary to construct a special absolute right to incorporeal property* in certain aspects – analogous to the right of ownership.[82]

So long as such a right has not been constructed, we are condemned to extend a number of norms of the right of ownership to paperless securities *by analogy*. Whereas norms concerning the right of ownership are capable of regulating the relations of people with regard to a *specific thing*, and conditionally one may speak about the admissibility of regulation with the assistance of these norms relations between

[82] The urgency of working out such is even greater considering that legislation in force knows only one type of incorporeal property – the "enterprise as a whole as a property complex" (Article 132(1), Civil Code) – with which the existence, effectuation, and transfer of a entire series of subjective civil rights are connected.

people in regard to the *aggregate of certain values* (possibly –
nonmaterial) with a sufficient degree of individualization of
which practice considers the expression of a quantity of these
values into certain absolute units (stocks or bonds), or money.
Moreover, one may suggest the paperless securities be
individualized by a reference to a legal fact – specific, sole,
and unrepeatable – whenever there are grounds for the arising
of subjective civil rights in paperless securities with the first
acquirer thereof. To be sure, in this event the registers of
possessors of securities are transformed into something similar,
as related in the English folktale "The House that Jack Built",
to:

And here – are five stocks of AO "Electrolampa",
Those very stocks
Which Vasia bought from Zhora,
Who had inherited them from Papa,
And Papa had exchanged them with a friend
There being forty-five
Of those very stocks
Which the friend bought from a girl friend,
Who was given them by her Mama,
Who had acquired them
During the process of privatization,
The Plant "Electrolampa"
Having issued them in 1993.

One may raise the question: why not change the concept
of the right of ownership itself? The term "right of ownership"
is remarkable, well-known, and signifies something more
complete and absolute – is something more required? Why
should it be traditionally accepted to use this term to designate
rights only and exclusively to things (material articles) – we
merely have to decide. One may indeed behave thus. But must
we do so?

Sometimes, from the standpoint of law, it would be desirable to combine the term "automobile" not only with the traditional "lorries" and "vans", but also to other vehicles on wheels – motorcycles, trailers, tractors, cranes, combines, carts, cars, mechanical loaders, hoists, and special self-propelled machinery (in the nature, for example, of agricultural or snow removal equipment), and so on. However, jurisprudence does not do this – it works out a special terminology (of the type "means of transport", "auto and motor means of transport", "mechanical means of transport", and so on). In our situation the situation is reversed: under "right of ownership" we combine, at a minimum, three heterogeneous essences – (1) the normal right of ownership, the right of ownership in the strict sense of the word; (2) exclusive rights, called "rights of intellectual property", and (3) rights to incorporeal essences – paperless securities and enterprises – as practice gravitates. Should the science of jurisprudence adapt itself to this? By no means.

We reiterate that legal science should serve practice, but not be the servant thereof! The role of legal science is to reflect life in a legal mirror; that is, in a description of life relations with the assistance of legal concepts and deriving conclusions concerning the rights and duties of person-participants of life relations. If the philistines take nothing – for legal terms they see only the words themselves and nothing more, then more is demanded from the scholar, for he is obliged to see beyond the terms, not merely slogans but also the essence of the concepts designated by them. The essence of absolute rights to material articles differs cardinally from the essence of an absolute right to ideal essences. In other words, the concepts concerning various absolute rights distinctive in their content by reason of dependence on the object whose conferment and alienation they formalize all the same should be objectively distinguished by what is not collected under the common slogan, which means to *objectively require a different terminological designation.* The science of jurisprudence also has worked out such designations; and not merely worked them out, but endured, one may say, many centuries of the pangs of birth. Today in jurisprudence we attempt to choose and sanitize. Why? Who will benefit from this? The penetration of dilettantism into science has always led to blundering and degeneration, and that we at present observe in the example of jurisprudence.

At the same time, practice is fully capable of enriching science. Whereas legal scholars deign to think over the processes that are occurring, if they are able to comprehend the essence of practical phenomena growing in the earth called paperless securities, if they can translate these phenomena into the language of jurisprudence, describe them in legal categories, will this not lead to the emergence of a new legal construction? Is it not simple for jurisprudence to give birth to one small baby together with the right of ownership and exclusive rights? It is another matter whether this is essential (see Chapter 8, below).

Thus, from the outset we established that modern practice considers paperless securities to be an object of the right of ownership, and also that certain legislative acts provide occasion for this. Next we learned that *to apply these prescriptions and understand existing practice literally was impossible* and established that one must proceed in the near future to the application *by analogy* of *certain* rules on the right of ownership to relations with regard to paperless securities, and in the long-term – to *construct a special absolute right to paperless securities.* Now we have received the explanation as to under what conditions the application by analogy is possible and the working out of a new absolute right – only provided that *by paperless securities is understood the ideal "something" that does not coincide with relative property rights.* Two conclusions flow from this:

(1) the institution of paperless securities used in practice

does not correspond to legislation in force and, from this point of view, those jurists who see in paperless securities only property rights, the application to them of norms concerning the right of ownership being considered to be utterly impossible, are correct. And existing practice is illegal since only *such* an understanding of the problem *has been written down within the legislative framework and traditional civilest canons*;

(2) on the other hand, jurists declaring paperless securities not to be rights themselves, but some sort of intellectual essence – "incorporeal things", "fictions", "aggregates", "complexes", and so on – are right because *such* a vision of paperless securities has been formed in modern practice *under the influence of the aspiration to crystallize and formalize the so-called right to a paperless security – a special absolute right built on the model of the right of ownership.* And here one does not see the unity of the essence of paperless securities with documentary – and here too is present the division of the right into an essence (ideal or material) and rights from an essence!

Why should *such* a division be created? With regard to the classical (documentary) security the answer is obvious: a paper document[83] makes possible treatment of the relative subject civil right consolidated therein not according to the rules of assignment of demands, but norms established for the acquisition and termination of the right of ownership. As regards paperless securities, the answer to the question "why?" is determined only by practical considerations: *practice still has not found a more effective means of defense of rights certified by paperless securities than the means built along the model of the vindicatio suit.* If another means will be found prescribed, on one hand, in legislation (understanding paperless securities as relative property rights) and, on the other, in the

---

[83] As also a document on a diskette, laser disc, and other material carrier since any individualized material essence (thing) may be the object of the normal, classical right of ownership, the right to the document.

canons of civilistics, separating from subjective rights of yet another incorporeal essence is virtually unnecessary.

The conventionality and frailty of modern practice also is to be discovered in another domain. The classical security (thing) is objective and realistic, accessible to the impact of all third persons without exception, all processes occurring within it, and also accessible directly to the uniform perception of all third persons. As a result a situation may occur which, taking advantage of the terminology of the law of mortgage, may be called a situation of *duplicity of fact and law*: a security (or thing) may prove to be with a person who has not formally legitimated it, and this means formally possessing the right arising from the security at a time when in fact the security may belong to another person. The classical example of such a situation is the stealing of a bearer security: in the eyes of all third persons with respect to the victim the thief is the *actual possessor of the security*, and, consequently, the creditor with respect to it (possessor of the right from the security), but in fact is neither one nor the other since he does not possess the *right to the security*. Briefly, a thing may objectively prove to be with a person who is not its owner; however, this does not eliminate the right of ownership thereto on the part of the other person, the possibility of the effectuation thereof, and, when necessary – defense by the last.

A paperless security is something which ideally also exists only insofar as it is imagined. The same is so of subjective civil rights and legal duties – these too are an ideal essence existing only in the human consciousness. The very roots of the word "right" presuppose that a subjective *right* may belong only to the empowered person; to whom a subjective right belongs, with whom the human consciousness links it – he is empowered. A *thing* may be situated with a person illegally; a *right* with a person not empowered – never. In creating side by side with a subjective right an artificial "something", with the location of which a particular person links a supposition

concerning the affiliation to this person of subjective rights we
artificially create the duplicity of the *visibility of the fact* and
right since the possessor of this very "something" may be
whomsoever to who it is advantageous. Possibly this means
also the illegal possessor thereof; that is, the person to whom
the right to the "something" in reality does not belong and
who, consequently, also has no rights arising from this
"something". A question: why artificially multiply similar
situations when having discarded the ideal "something" and
retained only the concept of relative subjective rights we make
them impossible in principle?

But it may not happen so, the reader undoubtedly asks,
for there may be irrefutable evidence that particular relative
subjective civil rights belong to one person at a time when in
fact they belong to another, only the last may not prove this?
He may. But here we have the duplicity of the classical, normal
fact (for example, in the form of an entry in a register), and
not the visibility of fact and right. The arising thereof is
inevitable, and from what angle of vision have we not
considered paperless securities. How to eliminate this? How
to eliminate the visibility of the situation in which a right
belongs to a person who ... is not the possessor thereof (to
whom it does not belong)? In essence the question confronts
us: *how to defend paperless securities which themselves are
understood as relative subjective civil rights*? We turn to a
consideration thereof.

Chapter 8: Suits Concerning Recognition, Or Is It
Impossible to Manage Without the Absolute Right to Ideal
Essences?

IT IS POSSIBLE, indeed. At least to date civilistics has managed
completely without this absolute right.

The notion of the existence of such a right was expressed
in doctrinal writings only, so far as we are aware, by M. M.
Agarkov. Considering the question as to whether an obligation
might be violated by a third person, he wrote as follows:

> Even if it is acknowledged that the existence of an
> obligation creates for each and every with respect to a
> creditor a duty to refrain from infringements which might
> deprive a creditor of the possibility to effectuate his right
> of demand against a debtor, then all the same it is
> essential to distinguish two different legal relations: (a)
> the relation between a creditor and debtor (a violation
> is possible only on the part of the debtor) and (b) the
> relation between a creditor and each and every (a
> violation is possible on the part of each and every). In
> the first instance we will have a legal relation of
> obligation, and in the second – a special absolute right.
> *We note here that Soviet civil law does not know such an
> absolute right*, although in individual instances a suit
> against a third person for losses also is permitted.[84]

In other words, in the first instance one is speaking of a
violation of the right of obligation itself, and in the other – *the
right to the particular right of obligation*.

As an example of such a violation Agarkov cited the
instance of a right arising with a person receiving alimony to

---

[84] M. M. Agarkov, *Обязательство по советскому гражданскому
праву* [Obligation Under Soviet Civil Law] (1940), p. 26.

demand compensation of losses from a person who killed the person paying alimony. In reality this example absolutely does not illustrate what has been said: the scholar himself indicated that the right to a right of obligation creates duties for each and every *with respect to the creditor*. The example cited by him concerns the impact on the person of the debtor, such obligation having a strictly personal character (alimony obligation). Remove from the obligation the alimony (strictly personal) character – and everything is in its place. So long as the debtors are not killed, there always will be a debtor to a creditor. It will be either an heir in priority, or ultimately the State. The actions of a person who kills debtors influence, according to the general rule, only the economic, but not the legal, aspect of the right of obligation and the right to a right of obligation.

How should the illustration be here? Perhaps that which was cited above: a seller who has sustained a road transport accident, was not ready on time, did not receive performance. His property loss is expressed in interest. Another example: a person as a result of delay was late for a train; that is, lost his right to demand performance of a contract of carriage; in other words, *ceased to be a creditor and incurred losses*. Not to grant to the unhappy victim the right to demand contributory compensation for this loss from his causer of harm would be, at the least, unjust. The impact must affect the active subject, the empowered person – only then may one speak of a violation of an absolute right *to a right*. Whether a stockholder stumbles when entering the hall for sessions of the general meeting because of a defect in the floor, as a result of which the opportunity to be present at the meeting is lost, or whether a power of attorney and instruction to transfer is forged of the possessor paperless securities and a transaction is concluded in his name, whether the holder of a bill of exchange stubs his toe on uncleared ice on the pavement as a result of which he is in a hospital and the period lapses for protesting the bill of exchange, or whether an advocate hurrying to a session is in an automobile accident, or whether documents legitimating it are stolen from the creditor, or whether a postal communication of the acceptor concerning the acceptance of an offer, or a communication of an owner concerning the wish to take advantage of a preferential right of purchase or of the protestor concerning the protest made of a bill of exchange is lost, or the telegraph distorts the communication of a creditor concerning the choice of the subject of performance in an alternative obligation – these are all examples of instances of impact *on a creditor* which lead or could lead to a diminution of his *rights to relative rights*. When one speaks of an impact exerted on the debtor, one may speak about the fault of third persons, or about the regressive responsibility thereof to the debtor, but not about a diminution of creditor rights.

With such extensive opportunities to apply the category of an "absolute right to a right", civilist science has existed successfully so far without this. It is understandable that this, of course, is not an argument, but nevertheless! We shall try to ascertain why this has happened?

For a moment we shall divorce ourselves from the modern day and model the following situation. Someone is plotting to illegally "take possession" of another's property rights. What must he do to accomplish this? Obviously, take possession of documents which certify the respective rights; for example, to steal a debt receipt, security, or example of a contract with all of the documents appended thereto. And, of course, fabricate evidence of the transfer of rights – formalize a contract of assignment of demand, endorsement, assignment inscription on a security, and/or perform a transfer (or transfer of securities to a deposit account or account in a register). We now remove ourselves from securities and turn to a contract, say – a contract of loan.

Some person turns to a borrower (who the borrower has never seen in his life) and demands the return of a loan.

Naturally, the borrower declares that he never was a creditor to him, and therefore does not repay the loan. The purported lender presents the contract of loan itself and a debt receipt issued at one to by the borrower in confirmation of receipt of the loan formalized in the name of another person. But at the same time the purported lender submits to the borrower also a contract of assignment of demand under which this very contracting party under the contract of loan assigned all rights from the contract to him, the person now presenting the demand. Of course, the contract of assignment was fabricated, and the contract and debt receipt was stolen from the lender; however, the borrower does not know this. This may be elicited both *until* the borrower, getting on with these documents, performs the obligations (repays the amount of the loan and pays the interest on it), and *after*. How should the lender be defended? What? His rights of a lender? But if the loan has been repaid, interest has been paid, the duties have been performed, and this means there are no more rights since the rights do not exist without duties; there remains merely a violated property interest. How should it be defended? In the example given, logically, of course, one should demand the amounts received by the swindler from the borrower, relying on the norms of the Civil Code concerning the causing of harm. But in order to approximate the situation to our "paperless securities", say that the lender for some reason simply considered vital not compensation of harm but restoration of his subjective rights. How could he achieve such restoration?

The first situation – defense of the *rights* of the lender already existing (that is, defense undertaken at the stage preceding the performance of duties of the borrower). Since the transaction of an assignment of demands has not been concluded, and the document submitted concerning assignment was forged, one may not consider that the rights of the lender passed to a new creditor. They continue to belong to the lender; however, the facts – the absence with the lender of documents concerning the right and existence of a contract of assignment on his side of a contract of assignment – testify otherwise. The classical duplicity of fact and right have been created. How may it be overcome? Evidently only by having received an assurance of public power that despite the existing facts, the right in reality belongs not to the new, but to the previous creditor, the lender. Such assurances in the form of a judicial act may be received only according to the results of the consideration of a *suit concerning recognition of a right*, the defendant with regard to which will act the fictitious "new creditor", and the plaintiff – the lender. In the course of the consideration of the case it will be established that the contract of assignment of the demand of the lender in reality was not signed, the signature placed on it (supposedly the lender) – is a forgery, and consequently there was no transaction, the rights were not transferred, and this means they in truth should be recognized for the lender.

The second situation – defense of the *property interest* of the lender – arises at the stage extending from the moment of performance of the obligations (or termination of rights). Can an act of public power restore the demand of the lender against the borrower? In no way. The borrower has performed his obligations one and is not at fault that the performance provided to be performed to the wrong person. To place on the borrower a new obligation without his will and consent would be contrary to the very concept of a civil right as the rights of free and legally autonomous subjects. What remains? Only to *recognize for the victim the right of the lender with respect to the person who by illegal (fraudulent) means received performance.* If a demand with the victim against the swindler all the same arises, the possibility to determine the regime of this demand – be it considered to be delictual, *condictio*, or contractual – is a matter for the victim. And if for some reasons it is advantageous to have a demand based on the contract of loan, why should such a possibility not be recognized for him? Once again everything comes up against a *suit concerning the recognition of a right*: yes, the victim did not sign the contract of loan with the swindler and the loan was not provided to him, but despite all this, relying solely on the fact that the swindler deprived the creditor of the possibility to realize the demand of the lender against the borrower, the court should declare that the swindler thereby acknowledged the debt of the borrower to the victim.

And so, a suit concerning recognition of a right. Without delving into theoretical details of the doctrine concerning suits of this type,[85] we merely noted that an *act of public recognition of a right* for a particular subject is, including also an act of recognition (or confirmation) by the State of such obligation, for *that person for whom the right is recognized, realized as an element of his civil legal personality* (or legal capacity).[86] It is beyond doubt that any citizen *may* (has the possibility to be) *be* a lender; it is equally undoubted that far from every citizen at a particular moment of time is *in reality* a lender. The task of a court considering a suit concerning the recognition of a right is similar to the task of establishing a legal fact: the court establishes whether the plaintiff truly realized the capacity belonging to him to create such a subjective civil right, or not? If it was realized – then has this right terminated (or does it continue to exist)? And, finally, if it continues to exist, does it belong to the plaintiff or to someone else? Positive answers to each of these three questions enable a decision to

---

[85] See V. M. Gordon, *Иски о признании* [Suits on Recognition] (Iaroslavl', 1906); E. A. Krasheninnikov and E. Ia. Motovilovker, *Установительное притязание как средство защиты охраняемого законом интереса* [An Established Claim as a Means of Defence of an Interest Protected by a Law] (Iaroslavl', 1990).

[86] In the science of civil law there exist several various views on the correlation of these categories. This is neither the time nor place to analyze these views; we observe only that we adhere to that according to which these categories are identical (or of equal significance).

be rendered concerning satisfaction of the suit concerning recognition (or to recognize for the plaintiff a particular subjective civil right).

We shall endeavor to apply the discourse above to the rights comprising paperless securities.

The first stage is – the *establishment of legal facts by a court* that would enable one to confirm that the plaintiff actually realized one of the elements of his civil legal capacity, in particular, acquired stocks (or the right to participate in affairs and capital) of a determined joint-stock society. The establishes that yes, in reality, such facts happened: the person concluded a contract of purchase-sale for stocks, paid for them by monetary means, and in good time was entered in the register of stockholders of the emittent.

We continue; one must be very attentive during all further discourse. If civil legal capacity is the capacity (or possibility) *to have* any subjective civil rights in general, including, consequently, also every determined, every specific, subjective right, then the *diminution of any subjective right is simultaneously both an infringement on this right itself and an infringement on his capacity* (the particular specific subjective right) *to have; that is, civil legal capacity*. If only the bearer of the duties corresponding to this right may infringe upon the subjective right itself, as already noted, then *each and every is in a state to infringe on legal capacity*. The interference of a third (person (a stranger to the relative civil legal relation) in the existence and course of the particular legal relation is *an infringement on the civil (or private) legal capacity of the persons participating therein*.

Here is the mystery of the phenomenon of the "unknown absolute right" similar to the right of ownership. First, it has long been known to everyone, and second, — it is not a right at all. What has been said should in no event be grounds for relegating us to the group of proponents of the conception in accordance with which legal capacity is also a distinctive subjective right. Legal capacity is an inalienable property of an essence recognized by society as a subject of a right, *a special social property of an essence*. Despite the instruction of society expressed in a legislative norm concerning the deeming of all people without exception to have legal capacity, individual persons may, disregarding such, ignore the legal capacity of particular individuals, including by the means described above (to make difficult the effectuation by them of subjective rights belong to them or even deprive them of such). Legal capacities as an inalienable social property correspond not to the duty of all and each to refrain from an infringement on such,[87] *but the absence of the possibility (or subjective right) to infringe on legal capacity*. The possibilities correspond not to a duty, not to the ought, but to an impossibility; from this point of view, *it is not obligatory that a duty correspond to every subjective right, but that rightlessness, the absence of a right, "non-right" directly correspond.*[88]

What has been said leads to the conclusion of the need to review the concept which seems once and forever to have been confirmed in science – the concept of a violation of law (or unlawful action). Not only *is an action unlawful* (or violating a subjective right) which comprises a violation of a legal duty corresponding to a subjective right, but also *which is committed by a person who does not have the right to perform a particular action or who has exceeded the limits of the right which he does have.* Perhaps more natural that

---

[87] The recognition of such a duty presupposes that such situations also may exist in which the right to limit someone in legal capacity is recognized for a person. However, such a subjective right may not be recognized for anyone, since it would exceed the limits of private-law relations, the relations of equal with equal.

[88] We acknowledge that this thesis is untraditional and requires verification and study in the future. However, the acceptance thereof, without especially sticking out from civilist canons, helps resolve the task put – to defend the holders of paperless securities.

"unlawful" means "rightless", that is, performed without a right (or beyond the limits of the right)? But no, the concept dominant in legal science about unlawfulness is the consideration thereof as a violation of a legal duty or even norms of objective right.[89] Such a situation may not be assessed other than as a *material omission of legal science* whose roots are possibly in the neglect by jurisprudence of logical methods and excessive attraction to the description of legislative constructions.

And so it has been ascertained that someone has realized his legal capacity, has become the possessor of an aggregate of property rights comprising paperless securities. The second stage is the necessity to ascertain *whether these rights exist at the moment of examination*: were they not effectuated and were they terminated on other grounds. The further actions of a court depend upon the answer to this question. Depending upon the answer to this question, the court determines what precisely it will defend – a property right continuing to exist, or a wounded property interest. If one refers to stockholder rights, it is clear that so long as a joint-stock society – the emittent of stocks – exists, stockholders exist and the rights of stockholders, and this means their recognition always is possible; the issue is only for whom precisely. The greater portion of difficulties connection with the defense of a property interest are removed in a situation concerning stocks.

But one can not fail to give attention to the fact that the rights of a stockholder are realized not at once, but gradually, in the course of time. Should one recognize for a victim the right to a dividend already received by the swindler? Or the right to participate in a general meeting which already has been held and, consequently, a right was was effectuated by the swindler? Here are illustrated the peculiarities of corporative rights: only the respective joint-stock society can

---

[89] The latter understanding of unlawfulness is, possibly, more productive in the sphere of public law.

be recognized as the subject of the corresponding duties. To place on the swindler the duty to conduct a general meeting or to pay dividends is impossible. We shall return to this problem in the course of considering the third step of the court considering a case concerning recognition.

As regards rights certified by bonds – the rights to demand determined monetary amounts, it is not subject to any doubt that the duties corresponding to these rights may be placed on any person, including a swindler. The situation here, consequently, is the same as that considered above (in the event of a forged signature on a contract of assignment).

The last stage of consideration of a suit concerning recognition of a right is the establishment of *to whom belongs the subjective right which once arose and continues to exist* – to the plaintiff, or to he who is entered according to the data of the depositary (or registrar). It is essential to clarify that here we do not confront the classical duplicity of fact and right which we encountered previously. We would face duplicity if it were possible to speak of *rights which should be and ... rights which really exist*, since in accordance with prevailing legislation the possessor of paperless securities (read – possessor of relative subjective civil rights) is considered to be that person in whose name the said rights have been registered by the depositary or registrar.[90]

This circumstance differs in principle from all others considered. The essence of *vindicatio* is demanding and obtaining *by the owner* of his thing from a person *having no rights whatsoever to it*. The grounds for the suit concerning recognition of the right of demand of a lender under a contract is the existence of such with the lender and the *absence of such with the fictitious "new creditor"*. Here we are in a strange and unusual situation: should the interest of a *person-right possessor* be preferred to the interest of a person *who does not possess the contested right but should possess such and would*

---

[90] Once again we recall the article by Shatalov, note 50 above.

possess it in the event of normal (lawful) behavior of third persons?

A suit concerning recognition in this stage is materially modified; the maximum that the court may say upon the completion thereof is that the registrar (or depositary) had no grounds to make changes in the entry in the personal account (or deposit account) with respect to the affiliation of the contested securities. These *should* continue to be entered in the account of the plaintiff and *should not* be entered in the account of the defendant.[91] In other words, the third stage of consideration of a suit concerning recognition of a right comprising a paperless security *may not be limited only to declaring the affiliation of the contested right.* If it already belongs to the plaintiff, which is confirmed by respective entries in the register or in the deposit account, the suit should simply be refused; if it does not belong to the plaintiff, the court should elucidate under what circumstances the plaintiff was deprived of the contested right and, having established the unlawfulness thereof – decide whether it would be just to rectify the consequences of the illegal actions. How to rectify? *To deprive* of the right that person who possesses it and *only after this to recognize* such for the plaintiff.

---

[91] In principle one fact, that the suit is brought not against the emittent of the contested paperless securities but against the person in whose account such were entered, may serve as grounds for refuting the classification of the suit being considered as a suit concerning recognition since only the contracting party of the plaintiff in legal relations requiring recognition may be the defendant with regard to a suit concerning recognition.

Chapter 9: Suit Concerning Restoration of the Situation Which Existed Before Violation of Legal Capacity

THE USE, of course, of the term "to recognize" is figurative. One refers not to recognition as such (since to recognize a right for someone is possible only on condition that such truly exists in the plaintiff), but about a qualitatively different phenomenon – *restoration of the situation which existed before the violation of legal capacity.*[92]

We reiterate that unlike the suit concerning recognition, the suit concerning restoration is presented not against the supposed contracting party of the legal relation to be recognized, but against the person who committed the unlawful action, against the person who exceeded the limits of rights, against the person who is "lawless". In addition, in a suit concerning restoration a court must pass through yet a fourth stage: to determine *whether the violated property interest of the victim deserves restoration or not.* Depending upon the answer to that question, the court by its power either restores the situation which existed before the violation of legal capacity or refuses to do so. Such a decision shall be executed in an elementary manner (in our situation, with paperless securities) – by means of annulment of the new, groundless entries made in accounts and *restoration of the former.* An obliged person

---

[92] Proposals concerning the application of this means of defence of rights comprising paperless securities already have been expressed in doctrinal writings. See Konovalov, note 42 above, p. 33; A. Sinenko, «Судебные споры с участием регистраторов» [Judicial Disputes with the Participation of Registrars], *Рынок ценных бумаг* [The Securities Market], no. 8 (1998), p. 83; Shatalov, note 50 above, p. 67. However, all these authors encountered obstacles in the application of this means which within the framework of knowledge and methods they used could not be overcome. We hope that the text below will remove these problems in some measure.

(or emittent) *does not suffer* from such restoration – the quantity of paperless securities issued by it into circulation does not change, the amount of its obligations is not increased, only the empowered persons change. The person at whose expense the situation is restored which existed before the violation of rights, if it suffers, does so *only on the grounds of a legal and substantiated judicial act that has entered into legal force.*

The grounds for applying restoration of the situation which existed before the violation of a right as a means of defence of legal capacity is the mention thereof in this capacity in Article 12 of the Civil Code. The fact that it is regarded chiefly as a consequence of the invalidity of transactions does not mean that this means of defense was deprived of a universal significance – otherwise it would simply not have been named in Article 12 of the Civil Code relating the means of defense of any subjective civil rights.

One may not regard as an obstacle to its application the fact that according to the terminology of the Civil Code the subject of restoration is the situation which existed before the violation of the subjective *right* (and not legal capacity). Above we established that any infringement against any subjective right is at the same time also against legal capacity; accordingly, all means of defense of subjective *rights*, according to the general rule, must be applied also to the defence of such an object as *"naked" legal capacity.*

Thus it seems that the means of defense of rights comprising paperless securities is a *suit concerning restoration of the situation which existed before the violation of a right.* Here the two following questions arise: (1) how to restore those rights which already were realized by the swindler in the time that has elapsed since the violation of rights by him comprising paperless securities before the restoration of the previous situation? (2) under what conditions is the satisfaction of such a suit admissible?

As regards the answer to the first question, in order to receive it we turn to one of the clearest examples of instances when this question acquires special acuteness and urgency. Say that during the period of his swindling "possession" of paperless stocks the swindler succeeded in voting at a general meeting of stockholders in order to decide particular questions. May the state be restored that existed before the adoption of such decisions? And if the decisions concerned the election of members of the council of directors or executive organs of the joint-stock society, may, relying upon the contested decisions concerning the election, all decisions of these organs be deemed to be invalid (or some of them) – the council of directors, board, a director? May one "break" transactions concluded in the name of the joint-stock society by a director, the decision concerning the election of whom was deemed to be invalid? A simple natural question has so many various aspects.

The judicial practice dominant today considers such restoration to be possible. And there is logic to this position: once stocks have left the possession of the registered person other than by his will, one may consider that they never left him at all, belongs to him always, despite the entry in the register of stockholders. Never left him and always belonged to him means the swindler who voted the stocks voted illegally, and if without his votes a particular decision could not have been taken by the meeting, it should be acknowledged that such a decision was not taken at all. Once it was not taken … And so on, to infinity.

All is correct. But, at the same time, strange. Why? The stockholders may suddenly with astonishment learn that they have been deluded for a long time, supposing that they possess the stocks of three issues – in fact one issue was made in all, and the fact that they adopted a second and third in reality did not happen since someone voted for the adoption of decisions concerning these issues who did not have the right to do so. Thanks to the restoration of one stockholder in his rights, thousands of others may be deprived of their rights. The joint-stock society, accordingly, will be faced with the necessity to refund to stockholders that which they contributed in payment of stocks of the second and third issue, which in turn may entail the necessity to reduce the charter capital of the society. As is well-known, the last can not be effectuated without the adoption of a respective decision at the meeting of stockholders and without recognition of determined rights for creditors (Article 60, Civil Code). Even though there are no creditors or the last may not demand anything, if there are such and the "unempowered" meetings elected persons to office in the management organs of the joint-stock society: the transactions concluded by the last may be contested, and this means one may not speak of there being no creditors.

Is this normal? From the standpoint of one person – the stockholder restored in his rights – possibly, yes. But from the viewpoint of the other stockholders, creditors, and, finally, the joint-stock society itself – by no means! Of what are all the enumerated persons guilty? Why thanks to the solemnity of the rights of one person should the rights of thousands of other persons be impinged, limited or terminated completely. Of course, it is not the quantity of persons since all are equal before the civil law; however, one need not forget that the rights of a stockholder are merely one aspect of his status. We put the question: why does a society recognise determined rights for a stockholder with respect to itself? Because it is presupposed that the stockholder will effectuate his rights as his power, but only in its own interest, but *in the interest of the entire joint-stock society as a whole and, indirectly, also in the interests of all (or at least the majority) of stockholders*. The stockholders are linked by a common purpose – the achievement of prosperity and the flourishing of the joint-stock society, which means that individual stockholders, proceeding from the interests of the society and to its benefit may not under any conditions be contested by other stockholders. What is the

difference who voted with regard to the "contested stocks" –
the stockholder or the swindler – if the last voted in the interests
of the society as a whole and the majority of other
stockholders?

We have mentioned earlier the theoretical obstacle to
such restoration. This obstacle can not be overcome. One can
not recognize that which does not exist. One can not recognize
that a right which is terminated by the effectuation thereof:
the right has terminated, it no longer exists, neither its
appearance nor its cherished duplicity, and this means to
recognize nothing. This same reflection operates with regard
to the suit concerning restoration: the restoration of the
previous situation occurs by means of the "return" to the victim
of existing and not endowing him with new rights in place of
those which terminated. The termination of rights here may
become assimilated to the perishing of an individually-
determined thing: just as in the last instance there is nothing to
vindicate, so in the first instance (if the rights have terminated)
there is nothing to return.

A legislative obstacle, however, exists to imparting
retroactive force to an act of restoration of rights. This is the
already repeatedly mentioned provision of legislation in force
that he who has been *registered* in this capacity is empowered
with regard to paperless securities. No judicial acts can wipe
out the immutable fact that within a determined interval of
time, say, from 5 February 1998 to 30 June 2000 an entry
existed in the stockholder register concerning the affiliation of
a determined quantity of paperless stocks to a determined
person. Say that subsequently a court obliged this entry to be
destroyed and the former one restored, but this was already
the *subsequent*. It is true that by a judicial act one may decree
that a male is a female, but this does not eliminate the fact that
he is male.

Just as by a decision to satisfy a *vindicatio* suit a court
does not destroy the fact that the owner for a certain period

did not possess a thing, so too in restoring a right a court notes willingly or not that there was a time when a plaintiff did not have such. Otherwise there would be noting to vindicate and restore.

The sole legislative support for the practice of restoring effectuated and, consequently, terminated rights comprising paperless securities is the application by analogy of Article 167(1) of the Civil Code that an invalid transaction is considered to be such (invalid) from the *moment of conclusion thereof* irrespective of whether it is null or contestable, since the time lapsed after its conclusion is contestable. In performance of obligations which arose from such a transaction a multiplicity of various actions may be performed at this time, but nonetheless they all are subject to being vacated on the simple grounds that they have been effectuated under that transaction which was deemed to be invalid, albeit subsequently, with retroactive force.

What may one say here? Only that such an analogy is without foundation. It is not necessary to forget that two persons, as a rule, participate in a transaction; rarely – more, but all of them combine for something common that binds them together and places them in a situation analogous to mutual responsibility. *Each of the participants of an invalid transaction, as a rule, is informed about those circumstances that may serve as grounds for contesting it.* Accordingly, if knowing about these circumstances persons conclude a transaction, they should not complain later if these circumstances lead come into play, are actualized, and the risk of invalidity caused by them is realized. Everything is otherwise in the event of restoration of rights with regard to paperless securities – depending upon the consequences of such restoration are the rights of too many persons alien to the causer of harm and to the victim stockholder.

In order to impart retroactivity to a judicial act concerning the invalidity of a transaction the exists an express legislative instruction – Article 167(1), of the Civil Code (and with a reservation, Article 167(3) of the same Code). There is nothing in legislation similar with regard to the question of restoration of rights.

The application of the restoration of rights as a consequence of an invalid transaction also does not lead to the desired result. We shall speak in greater detail about this at the end of the Chapter.

Finally, the term itself – restoration – etymologically presupposes the return of that which for a certain period did not exist. If we speak of the "restoration of a church", we want to say that some church actually existed but then decayed, or was destroyed, and in general ceased to exist. Ultimately, one referred to its restoration – the creation of what which sometime was but *at the moment of adoption of the decision concerning restoration does not exist*. The same with the "restoration of rights" – at one time the rights existed with the victim which comprised paperless securities and then (by virtue of the swindling actions of a third person) ceased to exist and the possessor thereof changed. Therefore, because at a particular moment these rights did not exist, the victim requrests these rights be restored to him; if they in reality were with him the entire time, he has filed a suit not concerning restoration, but recognition.

As regards the answer to the question concerning the conditions of satisfaction a suit concerning the restoration of diminished legal capacity by means of the restoration of subjective rights, it can be found in modern judicial practice. If the phrase "demand concerning restoration bears a *vindicatio* character" is interpreted in the sense that a *demand concerning the restoration of a wounded civil legal capacity shall be satisfied on those same conditions under which the vindicatio suit is satisfied*, virtually everything is in its place. We recall these conditions.

Just as property may be demanded and obtained from an acquirer not in good faith in all instances, so too *in all instances a suit concerning the restoration of a right is subject to satisfaction at the expense of the possessor thereof not in good faith.* Naturally, the lack of good faith must be proved by the interested party; that is, by the plaintiff with regard to a suit concerning the restoration of a right. At the expense of a *right-possessor in good faith* (and among them there may prove to be such) may be resotred in rights comprising paperless securities only when such changed possessor without the will of the victim (as in the example cited above – by means of swindling on the part of a third person) or were received by the acquirer without compensation (for example, under a transaction of gift or by inheritance)(Article 302(1) and (2), Civil Code).

Above, however, we said that in their place stand not all, but "virtually all". We had in view Article 302(3) of the Civil Code, according to which money and bearer securities may not in general be demanded and obtained from an acquirer in good faith, and also – to the norm of Article 16 of the Statute on Bills of Exchange of virtually identical content. Of course, there are no grounds to extend these norms directly to paperless securities as this is obstructed by the exclusive *inscribed* character of paperless securities[93] (we have not spoken about the possibility of the existence of order paperless securities – in practice so far there are no such). But this is entirely natural

---

[93] It is curious that the Provisional Statute in force previously on keeping the register of possessors of inscribed securities, confirmed by Decree of the Federal Securities Commission of 12 July 1995, No. 3 (*Экономика и жизнь* [The Economy and Life], no. 32 (1995)) established in point 3.1.7(4) that one may not demand and obtain from an acquirer in good faith inscribed securities as well. Since with respect to documentary securities this provision was contrary to Article 302 of the Civil Code, it should have been applied exclusively to the institution of paperless securities. See Belov, «Защита интересов ...», note 13 above, p. 36.

since subjective rights – and paperless securities are property rights – in general may not exist without linkage to the name of their possessor. In other words, if documentary securities may be not only inscribed, but also order and even bearer, then paperless securities do not allow such spaciousness to themselves. As for the inscribed character of paperless securities – a compulsory phenomenon objectively conditioned – does it make sense to consider an extension by analogy to them of Article 302(3) of the Civil Code? If it is true that the institution of paperless securities was thought up in order to increase the speed and stability of the turnover of property rights, then insofar as this purpose is served by Article 302(3) of the Civil Code is it not logical to combine the efforts of both institutions operating in a single direction? It proves to be otherwise, that there is no difference at all between the turnover of rights comprising the content of paperless securities and the turnover of other rights.

Russian judicial practice is frankly mistaken and fallacious in considering to be a necessary condition of the restoration of rights to paperless securities the deeming invalid of transactions which served as the grounds for their transition from the victim to the possessor. If a *vindicatio* suit is satisfied irrespective of deeming transactions to be invalid under which property passed to the defendant, and the demand concerning restoration of property rights is of a *vindicatio* character, it is entirely logical to permit the satisfaction thereof irrespective of the validity of the grounds of the transfer of paperless securities. In addition, as practice shows, the contesting of transactions not only does not always lead to a cherished aim, but is impossible. What transaction should a victim contest when paperless stocks were withdrawn from his personal account in the register of stockholders under an instruction of transfer containing a forgery of his (the plaintiff) signature? The very "giving of the instruction of transfer"? But can this act in general be considered to be a transaction, and moreover in a situation when it was signed by an unempowered person? Should not one rather say that there was in general no transaction at all. But if this be so, what then should be contested? The question of what to contest is urgent in another situation – when the acquirer of paperless securities calls his right not a transaction, but another grounds, say, an act of acceptance of an inheritance as the heir by operation of law, by a judicial or administrative act, and, finally, by the actions of the emittent(with regard to the converting, splitting, or consolidation of stocks). What, on what grounds, and according to what rules should be contested in such situations?

One must recall that even if there are grounds for contesting the first transaction (say, between the victim and swindler), this does not mean the automatic invalidity of all subsequent transactions. Perhaps one may see in the first transaction some flaw, say, to declare it not to correspond to the requirements of a law.[94] But what will be unlawful in the next transaction – concluded between two persons in good faith – by the alienator and the new acquirer of paperless securities? How is the plaintiff to receive information at all concerning which transaction he should contest? And under what article should be contest the transaction with which he has no relation? A plaintiff can not be satisfied with some intermediate result – he needs the paperless securities, the absence of which with the defendant in a suit concerning the invalidity of a consecutive transaction deprives the suit of any sense because the application of bilateral restitution desired by the plaintiff will not occur – the defendant will only

---

[94] Although to do this is not simple since illegal actions are committed only by one party under the transaction (swindler); the other party may be completely in good faith. Attention has been drawn repeatedly to this in the specialist literature. See Gorbikov and Baranov, note 13 above, p. 94; Sinenko, note 92 above, p. 83.

contributorily compensate him for the value of the stocks sold
and the plaintiff, respectively, will return the money received
from the defendant.[95] Sense? The most impracticable variant
is received.

* * *

And so: a suit concerning the restoration of the situation
that existed before the violation of a right. We report that such
a name for the suit says nothing about its legal nature. The
question is the more urgent since it is obvious from the above
that a suit concerning the restoration of the situation which
existed before the violation of rights comprising paperless
securities can not be reduced to a suit concerning recognition.
Nor is it a suit concerning awarding since it does not pursue
the aim of compelling the defendant to perform any actions to
the benefit of the plaintiff; the very essence of relations
predetermining the impossibility of the restoration of rights
comprising paperless securities without the participation of a
third person (registrar) obstructs this. What remains? The
classical dominant procedural theory does not know other
types of suits to be singled out with regard to means of defense
of rights and interests.[96] It remains to remember the side shoots
of Russian procedural science – transformation suits. Once

---

[95] See Gorbikov and Baranov, note 13 above, p. 94; Sinenko, note 92
above, p. 83. So that this does not happen, the last proposes to restore the
situation which existed before the violation of the right "... by means of
obliging the defendant to acquire on the market the necessary quantity of
securities and transfer them to the ownership of the plaintiff". Marvelous,
only this is not restoration of the situation, but the contributory
compensation of losses in kind.

[96] G. L. Osokina, *Иск: Теория и практика* [The Suit: Theory and
Practice] (2000), pp. 69-70.

[97] See Osokina, note 96 above, pp. 71-82 and the literature specified
there; also see Krasheninnikov, «К теории преобразовательных исков»
[Towards a Theory of Transformation Suits], in *Роль права в деле*

again, confining ourselves to a reference to the specialist literature,[97] we add up the results: a suit concerning the restoration of the situation of a person deprived of paperless securities is the *classical transformation suit*, the subject of which is the *transformation of a legal relation by means of substitution of the active participant thereof* (stockholder and/ or creditor).

повышения благосостояния советских граждан в свете решений XXVII съезда КПСС [The Role of Law in the Cause of Enhancing the Well-Being of Soviet Citizens in Light of Decisions of the XXVII Congress of the Communist Party of the Soviet Union] (Tartu, 1987), I; id, «О субъектном составе преобразовательных правоотношений» [On the Subject Composition of Transformation Legal Relations], in *Вопросы теории охранительных правоотношений* [Questions of the Theory of Protective Legal Relations] (Iaroslavl', 1991); id, «Преобразовательное притязание как средство защиты охраняемого законом интереса» [Transformation Claim as a Means of Defence of an Interested Protected by a Law], in *Материально-правовые и процессуальные средства охраны и защиты интересов государства и общества* [Material-Legal and Procedural Means of the Protection and Defence of the Interests of State and Society (Kalinin, 1988).

Afterword

SINCE THIS entire book has been orientated towards
practitioners and in the service of practical tasks, in all
likelihood it will not be a greater transgression to turn in the
final pages towards my immediate colleagues – legal scholars.
The style of conducting a polemic by the proponents of the
subjective-rights theory has left a strange impression with me.
All is done so that the outcome is known in advance. Thus
behave pupils driving a decision towards an answer known
beforehand: this is not said, but I will all my powers will
endeavor to receive that result, and therefore this is written in
a textbook. Not because I wish to seek out a path towards the
truth, but because this is necessary.

Take one example. Korshunova needs to prove that a
document is not a material bearer of official information, but
is the *information itself*, it not being important on what carrier
it is fixed. In her aspiration Korshunova omitted to use the
provisions of Article 2 of the Federal Law of 20 February
1995, No. 24-ФЗ "On Information, Informatization, and the
Defense of Information".[98] The argument is rather inflexible:
such is the law! But what is the result of the use of such an
"argument"? An interesting scholarly article proved to be filled
with propositions having nothing in common not only with
theory and the remnants of legislation, but also with practice.
Suffice it to say that the author was compelled to resort to the
use of expressions of the type "document of a security",
"document of a paperless security"; "requisites of securities
of the paperless form", "information represented by the
document itself", "presentation of information", and so on.[99]
– expressions encountered nowhere else (including in
legislation). Korshunova should sense that something is not

[98] *СЗ РФ* (1995), no. 8, item 609.
[99] Korshunova, note 4 above, pp. 50-51.

right, that she has done nothing new, merely taken to the absurd an approach chosen by a law – but no! Nothing of the sort! In her conception her thoughts succeeded in achieving heretofore unattained legal heights.

Here is an example from Korshunova herself. "... Securities in paperless form are not a new institution in civil law ... They all the same may be relegated to classical securities, although today ... in defense of rights certified by a paperless security it is so far impossible to apply the rights to a thing means of defense.[100] Serious propositions! How are they substantiated? The grounds are concealed under the first two marks of omission; they are brief, and therefore the reader does not become fatigued if we allow them to be quoted in full: "I suggest that ..." and "I think that ...". Remarkable, is it not?

Another author, Krylova, in her aspiration to prove that even normal classical securities are not in essence a thing,[101] not ashamed to encroach even on the principle of presentation (or transfer) and the primacy of the right to a security over the right from a security – immutable postulates of the theory of securities which have withstood many centuries of verification. How did she succeed? Very simple: the first she declared to be a fact occurring only "in certain instances", and the second – a consequence of the unhappy formulation of the Federal Law on the Securities Market.[102] The matter was brought to completion by a quotation cited by her from Agarkov, from which it became clear: the author simply had

---

[100] Korshunova, note 4 above, p. 53.

[101] In principle this thesis all proponents of the subjective-rights theory of securities try to vindicate, but the attempts to prove it are virtually undertaken by no one. For example, the entire work of Iuldashbaeva is built on it; however, the evidence there is ... several quotations from the works of various scholars and a reference to Anglo-American law with its "broad" concept of the right of ownership. See Iuldashbaeva, note 12 above, pp. 10-15.

[102] See Krylova, note 4 above, pp. 62, 63.

not analyzed in essence the classical theory of securities and (presumably) did not attempt to do so. The last circumstances caused in us a feeling of squeamishness, forced us to reject attempts to discover any sense in her pseudo-scientific reflections, and declare shame on an ignoramus of jurisprudence!

Certain works – for example, the voluminous work of Murzin, or the lengthy article of Demushkina – we already have had the honour to characterize.[103]

One may summarize what has been said as follows. In publications of the proponents of the conception of paperless securities as securities one may find whatever one wishes, but one does not feel in them that which is most important – inspiration and professionalism. The last is understandable – pseudo-science can never be built on scientific postulates. But the first? After conversations "heart to heart", we are confirmed in the view that: the *conception in reality is defended insincerely*. Brief meditations helped find the reasons which explain this situation.

The fact is that at one time, in 1989-1993, that is, when the institution of paperless securities in Russia was only just standing on its feet, *no one* (we stress – **no one**!) *doubted that this is normal, legal, and substantiated*. The conflict of norms of the 1991 Fundamental Principles of Civil Legislation and the Statute on the Issue and Circulation of Securities and Stock Exchanges was simply not noted because the Fundamental Principles, as an all-union act and not "purely Russian" was frankly ignored. Only when working out the draft Civil Code of the Russian Federation was it elicited that there turned out to be a problem.[104]

The earliest publications which settled the right of

---

[103] On Murzin, see above; on Demushkina, see Belov, «Юридическая природа ...», no. 5 (1997), pp. 23-26; no. 6, pp. 49-52.

[104] The first publication in time raising this problem was Belov, «О безналичной форме ...» note 13 above, p. 5, signed with the pseudonym "S. Rudzinskii". A year later criticial remarks addressed towards

paperless securities to exist were brief articles by practitioners from the young Russian stock market – brief, if not to say, scraps, but all the same, bold, complacent, and caustic.[105] It is clear to all that paperless securities are as natural a phenomenon as may be in the world! Only the compilers of the draft Civil Code, ossified in their socialist preconceptions, for some reason do not want to understand this. Pseudo-scholars of today became entangled at the time in what is called "not thinking", "not being orientated" – neither commercial people nor scholars were supported, that is, tacitly agreed with the entire reality contemporary to them, including also to lump everything together as "non-cash securities". Although from the standpoint it is not convenient to dispute the classic and ask: and where were you earlier with your "documents-securities"?! Why was the head of the paperless hydra not cut off in time? It is better to pretend, to declare that "It was

---

cont'd
"paperless securities" were expressed by E. A. Sukhanov, «Ценные бумаги: Мировая практика и российское новаторство» [Securities: World Practice and Russian Innovation], *Экономика и жизнь* [Economy and Life], no. 15 (1994), p. 22; and two years later, Krashenninikov, note 4 above, p. 7, including the footnote, pp. 11-12.

[105] See, for example, A. Volkov and A. Privalov, «Кодекс не в чести» [Not a Code of Honour], *Коммерсант* [Kommersant], no. 37 (1994), pp. 14-15; A. Kozlov, A. Semin, and B. Cherkasskii, «Ценные бумаги: сделки, регистрация, реестр, депозитарий» [Securities: Transactions, Registration, Register, Depositary], *Экономика и жизнь: Экономическая газета* [The Economy and Life: Economic Newspaper], no. 2 (1994), p. 22; A. Kozlov, A. Semin, B. Cherkasskii, and E. Demushkina, «Операции с ценными бумаги: Основные понятия» [Securities Operations: Basic Concepts], *Экономика и жизнь: Ваш партнер* [The Economy and Life: Your Partner], no. 13 (1994), p. 9; no. 14, p. 9; A. Kozlov, «Депозитарий, реестродержатель, регистратор сделок с ценными бумагами: кто главнее, что важнее?» [Depositary, Register-Holder, Registrar of Securities Transactions: Who is Higher: What is More Important?], *Экономика и жизнь: Ваш партнер* [The Economy and Life: Your Partner], no. 23 (1994), p. 9; no. 24, p. 9.

intended thus", and, continuing aloud with soap in one's mouth
to try to vindicate paperless securities and internally continue
to wonder at oneself: this is what the human mind was invented
for and nature so resourceful.

There are two more reasons that give offence to some
colleagues. One can not, however, fail to mention them.

The view widely shared in the world of scholarship that
in the doctrine of securities-documents everything has been
accomplished, all summits conquered, and islands discovered.
If the canons, postulates, and constructions are not the simplest
– one must study everything and take them into account in
own researches. One may write about paperless securities with
virtually a clean sheet – there are not canons, no constructions.
Take the Law on securities or the Statute on the Federal
Securities Commission and onward! In a couple of hours a new
"theory" is ready. In other words, the *temptation* is very, very
great to *occupy oneself* with *quasi-scientific speculations* – this
is the first reasons which, of course, is no credit to scholars but
may be explained and forgiven.

The second reason is the temptation of a lackey worship
of science over practice. It is beyond doubt that science must
rely on practice; its problems are the guiding star of science.
But when scholars cease to serve the cause and begin to serve
persons (and today almost no one lives on scholarly earnings
– this is a secret to no one), engaging in scholarship is
reminiscent of engaging in prostitution. An employer needs
someone to defend his interests in a dispute with the registrar
– we write a "scholarly article" as to how this may be done.
Courts vindicate paperless securities? It is noteworthy, we will
vindicate! One is dismissed and goes to work at a registrar –
and bang! On the judge's table lies an "expert opinion" that
only things may be the subject of vindication. *It is so convenient,
so practical, so advantageous – that is the second reason, very
distressing, since one can neither understand nor forgive such
behavior.*

Bibliography of Sources Used

Агарков, М. М. *Обязательство по советскому гражданскому праву* [The Obligation Under Soviet Civil Law] (М., 1940).

___. *Учение о ценных бумагах* [Doctrine on Securities] (М., 1927); republished – М., 1993; М., 1994).

Алехин, Б. «Метаморфозы трансфер-агента и регистратора» [Metamorphoses of the Transfer Agent and Registrar], *Рынок ценных бумаг* [Securities Market], no. 17 (1996), pp. 35-36.

Андреев, В. К. *Рынок ценных бумаг: Правовое регулирование. Курс лекций* [The Securities Market: Legal Regulation. Course of Lectures]. (М., 1998).

Белевич, А. В. «Ценные бумаги как объекты гражданского права. Эмиссионные ценные бумаги» [Securities as Objects of Civil Law. Emission Securities], in А. Е. Шерстобитов (ред.), *Правовые основы рынка ценных бумаг* [Legal Foundations of the Securities Market] (М., 1997), pp. 71-83.

Белов, В. А. «Защита интересов добросовестного приобретателя ценных бумаг», [Defence of Interests of Good-Faith Acquirer of Securities], *Законодательство* [Legislation], no. 6 (1997), pp. 33-39.

___. «Комментарий к статье И. Горбинкова и Ю. Баранова 'Как защитить права собственников именных ценных бумаг'» [Commentary on the Article by I. Gorbinkov and Iu. Baranov, 'How to Defend the Rights of Owners of Inscribed Securities'], *Рынок ценных бумаг* [Securities Market], no. 13 (1997), p. 95.

___. *Ценные бумаги в российском гражданском праве* [Securities in Russian Civil Law] (М., 1996).

___. *Ценные бумаги как объекты гражданских прав: Вопросы теории* [Securities as Objects of Civil Rights] (М., 1996).

Диссертация ... к. ю. н. в форме научного доклада, выполняющего также функции автореферата.

___. «Юридическая природа 'бездокументарных ценных бумаг' и 'безналичных денежных средств'» [Legal Nature of 'Paperless Securities' and 'Non-Cash Monetary Means'], *Рынок ценных бумаг* [Securities Market], no. 5 (1997), pp. 23-26; no. 6, pp. 49-52.

Волков, А., Привалов, А. «Кодекс не в чести» [Not an Honour Code], *Коммерсант* [Kommersant], no. 37 (1994), pp. 14-15.

Габов, А., Яни, П. «Арест ценных бумаг по уголовному делу» [Arrest of Securities Under Criminal Law], *Росссийская юстиция* [Russian Justice], no. 8 (1999).

Горбиков, И., Баранов, Ю. «Как защитить права собственников именных ценных бумаг» [How to Defend Rights of Owners of Inscribed Securities], *Рынок ценных бумаг* [Securities Market], no. 13 (1997), pp. 94-95.

Гордон, В. М. *Иски о признании* [Suits Concerning Recognition]. (Iaroslavl, 1906).

Демушкина, Е. С. «Безналичные ценные бумаги – фикция или реальность?» [Non-Cash Securities – Fiction or Reality?], *Рынок ценных бумаг* [Securities Market], no. 18 (1996), pp. 68-72; no. 19, pp. 22-26; no. 20, pp. 68-69.

Дробышев, П. Ю. «Бездокументарный вексель: юридическая конструкция и право на существование» [Paperless Bill of Exchange: Legal Construction and Right to Existence], *Рынок ценных бумаг* [Securities Market], no. 17 (1996), pp. 8-9.

Есаулкова, Т. «Конвертация акций российских эмитентов в АДР» [Converting of Stocks of Russian Emittents into ADRs], *Рынок ценных бумаг* [Securities Market], no. 9 (1998), pp. 8-9.

Ефимова, Л. «Правовой режим бездокументарных ценных бумаг», [Legal Regime of Paperless Securities], *Закон* [Law], no. 7 (1997).

____. «Правовые проблемы безналичных денег» [Legal Problems of Non-Cash Money], *Хозяйство и право* [The Economy and Law], no. 1 (1997), pp. 28-39; no. 2, pp. 39-49.

Канн, С. Ю. *Защита прав владельцев ценных бумаг* [Defence of Rights of Possessors of Securities] (М., 2000). Автореферат дис. … к.ю.н.

Козлов, А. «Депозитарий, реестродержатель, регистратор сделок с ценными бумагами: кто главнее, что важнее?» [Depositary, Register-Holder, Registrar of Securities Transactions: Who is Higher, What Is More Important?], *Экономика и жизнь: Ваш партнер* [The Economy and Life: Your Partner], no. 23 (1994); p. 9; no. 24, p. 9.

____., **Семин, А., Черкасский, Б.** «Ценные бумаги: сделки, регистрация, реестр, депозитарий» [Securities: Transactions, Registration, Register, Depositary], *Экономика и жизнь: Экономическая газета* [The Economy and Life: Economic Newspaper], no. 2 (1994), p. 22.

____., **Семин, А., Черкасский, Б., Демушкина, Е.** «Операции с ценными бумагами: Основные понятия» [Securities Operations: Basic Concepts], *Экономика и жизнь: Ваш партнер* [The Economy and Life: Your Partner], no. 13 (1994), p. 9; no. 14, p. 9.

Коновалов, В. «Об ответственности специализированного регистратора» [On the Responsibility of a Specialized Registrar], *Рынок ценных бумаг* [Securities Market], no. 3 (1998), pp. 32-33.

Коршунова, Ж. В. «Правовой режим безбумажных ценных бумаг» [Legal Regime of Paperless Securities], in *Актуальные проблемы науки и практики коммерческого права: Сборник научных трудов* [Urgent Problems of Science and Practice of Commercial Law: Collection of Scientific Works] (Spb., 2000), III, pp. 49-60.

Котов, О. «Сделки с акциями на внебиржевом рынке: проблемные вопросы» [Stock Transactions on the Over the Counter Market: Problem Questions], *Рынок ценных бумаг*

[Securities Market], no. 9 (1998), pp. 72-74.

Крашенинников, Е. А. «К теории преобразовательных исков» [Towards a Theory of Transformatio Suits], in *Роль права в деле повышения благосостояния советских граждан в свете решений XXVII съезда КПСС* [The Role of Law in the Cause of Increasing the Well-Being of Soviet Citizens in Light of Decisions of the XXVII Congress of the Communist Party of the Soviet Union] (Tartu, 1987), I.

___. «О субъектном составе преобразовательных правоотношений» [On the Subject Composition of Transformation Legal Relations], in *Вопросы теории охранительных правоотношений* [Questions of the Theory of Protection Legal Relations] (Iaroslavl' 1991).

___. «Преобразовательное притязание как средство защиты охраняемого законом интереса» [Transformation Claim as Means of Defence of Interest Protected by Law] in *Материально-правовые и процессуальные средства охраны и защиты интересов государства и общества* [Material-Legal and Procedural Means of Protection and Defence of Interests of State and Society] (Kalinin, 1988).

___. *Ценные бумаги на предъявителя* [Bearer Securities] (Iaroslavl', 1995).

___., **Мотовиловкер, Е. Я.** *Установительное притязание как средство защиты охраняемого законом интереса* [Established Claim as Means of Defence of Interested Protected by Law] (Iaroslavl', 1990).

Крылова, М. «Ценная бумага – вещь, документ или совокупность прав?» [Security Thing, Document, or Aggregate of Rights?], *Рынок ценных бумаг* [Securities Market], no. 2 (1997), pp. 60-63; no. 4, pp. 57-60; no. 5, pp. 29-32.

Лысихин, И. «Давайте разберемся в дефинициях», [Let's Analyze Definitions], *Рынок ценных бумаг* [Securities Market], no. 17 (1996), pp. 37-40.

___. «Удостоверение и реализация прав по эмиссионным

ценным бумагам» [Certification and Realization of Rights Under Emission Securities], *Рынок ценных бумаг* [Securities Market], no. 18 (1996), pp. 64-65.

Марченко, А. «Символ комплекса прав» [Symbol of Complex of Rights], *Рынок ценных бумаг* [Securities Market], no. 12 (1996), p. 14.

Мурзин, Д. В. *Ценные бумаги – бестелесные вещи. Правовые проблемы современной теории ценных бумаг* [Securities – Incorporeal Things. Legal Problems of the Contemporary Theory of Securities] (M., 1998).

Нерсесов, Н. О. *О бумагах на предъявителя с точки зрения гражданского права* [On Bearer Securities from the Standpoint of Civil Law] (M., 1889).
    Reissued in 1998 and 2000 in the Series "Classics of Russian Civilistics".

Окунев, К. «Феномен бездокументарной ценной бумаги» [The Phenomenon of the Paperless Security], *Кодекс-INFO: Информационный бюллетень текущего законодательства* [Kodeks-INFO: Information Bulletin of Current Legislation], no. 18 (1996).

Осокина, Г. Л. *Иск: Теория и практика* [The Suit: Theory and Practice] (M., 2000).

Рудзинский, С. [Белов, В. А.]. «О безналичной форме выпуска ценных бумаг» [On the Non-Cash Form of Issue of Securities], *Бизнес и банки* [Business and Banks], no. 35 (1993), p. 5.

Рыжков, О. «Выпуск ценных бумаг: сначала права, затем бумаги» [Issue of Securities: First the Rights, Next the Securities], *Рынок ценных бумаг* [Securities Market], no. 17 (1996), pp. 51-53.

Синенко, А. «Судебные споры с участием регистраторов» [Judicial Disputes With the Participation of Registrars], *Рынок ценных бумаг* [Securities Market], no. 8 (1998), pp. 80-85.

Сперанский, В. «Бездокументарные ценные бумаги» [Paperless Securities], *Российская юстиция* [Russian Justice], no. 4 (1998).

Суханов, Е. А. «Вступительная статья» к книге *Ценные бумаги в российском гражданском праве* [Introduction to *Securities in Russian Civil Law*](М., 1996), pp. 3-16.

___. «Ценные бумаги: Мировая практика и российское новаторство» [Securities: World Practice and Russian Innovation], *Экономика и жизнь: Экономическая газета* [The Economy and Life: Economic Newspaper], no. 15 (1994), p. 22.

Трофименко, А. «Признаки ценной бумаги» [Indicia of a Security], *Российская юстиция* [Russian Justice], no. 7 (1997).

___. «Споры о ценных бумагах» [Disputes Concerning Securities], *Российская юстиция* [Russian Justice], no. 6 (1998).

Трусова, О. «Некоторые вопросы правового регулирования залога ценных бумаг» [Certain Questions of the Legal Regulation of the Pledge of Securities], in *Актуальные* проблемы науки и практики коммерческого права: Сборник научных трудов [Urgent Problems of the Science and Practice of Commercial Law: Collection of Scholarly Works] (Spb., 2000), pp. 94-106.

Шаталов, А. «Депонент и депозитарий: Вот тебе, бабушка, и Юрьев день» [Depositor and Depositary: Here's to You, Grandmother, and Iur'ev Day], *Рынок ценных бумаг* [Securities Market], no. 2 (1997), pp. 64-65.

___. «Как защитить права на бездокументарные ценные бумаги» [How to Defend Rights to Paperless Securities], *Рынок ценных бумаг* [Securities Market], no. 20 (1996), pp. 66-67.

Юлдашбаева, Л. Р. *Правовое регулирование оборота эмиссионных ценных бумаг (акций, облигаций)* [Legal Regulation of Turnover of Emission Securities (Stocks, Bonds)] (М., 1999).

Яковлев, В. И. *Регулятивные и охранительные правоотношения в сфере рынка ценных бумаг в России*

[Regulatory and Protective Legal Relations in Sphere of the Securities Market] (М., 1999). Автореферат дис. ... к.ю.н.

Яроцкий, В. «Риск в правоотношениях по ценным бумагам» [Risk in Legal Relations With Regard to Securities], *Российская юстиция* [Russian Justice], no. 7 (2000).

The items preceding are those principally "used" in preparing the basic text and footnotes. We could not, of course, omit to mention the classic works by M. M. Agarkov and N. O. Nersesov, for without them there would be no classical theory of securities, of which we are an adherent. Naturally, these works are far from all of those which have appeared on the problem in recent years. Among other publications are:

Алехин, Б. И. *Рынок ценных бумаг: Введение в фондовые операции* [The Securities Market: Introduction to Exchange Operations] (Samara, 1992).

Андреев, В. К. «Проблема правового регулирования рынка ценных бумаг» [The Problem of Legal Regulation of the Securities Market], *Государство и право* [State and Law], no. 3 (1997), pp. 86-93.

Butler, W. E., Gashi-Butler, M. E. *Корпорации и ценные бумаги в России и США* [Corporations and Securities in Russia and the United States] (М., 1997).
Text in English and in Russian.

Бушев, А. Ю. *Акции по законодательству Российской Федерации* [Stocks Under Legislation of the Russian Federation] (Spb., 1997). Автореферат дис. ... к. н. д.

Голубков, А. Ю. «Правовое регулирование рынка ценных бумаг» [Legal Regulation of the Securities Market], *Государство и право* [State and Law], no. 2 (1997), pp. 103-108.

Демушкина, Е. «Становление системы безналичных ценных бумаг в России: правовые проблемы» [Origin of the System of Non-Cash Securities], *Экономика и жизнь* [The Economy and Life], no. 25 (1995).

Крашепинников, Е. А. «О легальных определенных ценных бумаг» [On Legal Determined Securities], *Правоведение* [Jurisprudence], no. 4 (1992), p. 35-39.

Майфат, А. В. «Ценные бумаги (сравнительный анализ понятий в правовых системах России и США)» [Securities (Comparative Analysis of Concepts in the Legal Systems of Russia and the USA) *Государство и право* [State and Law], no. 1 (1997), pp. 83-91.

Миркин, Я. М. *Ценные бумаги и фондовой рынок* [Securities and the Stock Exchange] (M., 1995).

Треушников, М. К. (ред.). *Формы защиты прав инвесторов в сфере рынка ценных бумаг* [Forms of Defence of the Rights of Investors in the Sphere of the Securities Market] (M., 2000).

Фельдман, А. А., Лосутов, А. Н. *Российский рынок ценных бумаг* [The Russian Securities Market] (M., 1997).

Шорс, М. «Правовая база фондового рынка: состояние и изменения», [Legal Base of the Stock Market: State and Changes], *Деловой экспресс* [Business Express], 20 February 1996.

Юлдашбаева, Л. «Правовая природа бездокументарных ценных бумаг», [The Legal Nature of Paperless Securities], *Хозяйство и право* [The Economy and Law], no. 10 (1997).

FEDERAL LAW ON THE SECURITIES MARKET

[Federal Law No. 39-ФЗ, 20 March 1996,
as amended by Federal Law No. 182-ФЗ, 26 November
1998, Federal Law No. 139-ФЗ, 8 July 1999, Federal Law
No. 121-ФЗ, 7 August 2001, and Federal Law No. 185-ФЗ,
28 December 2002. СЗ РФ (1996), no. 17, item 1918; (1998),
no. 48, item 5857 (1999), no. 28, item 3472; (2001), no. 33(I),
item 3424; (2002), no. 52(II), item 5141]

Section I. General Provisions

Chapter 1. Relations Determined by Present Federal Law

Article 1. Subject of Regulation of Present Federal Law

Relations which arise during the emission and circulation of emission securities, irrespective of the type of emitent,
when circulating other securities in instances provided for by
federal laws, and also the peculiarities of the creation and activity of professional participants of the securities market, shall
be regulated by the present Federal Law [as amended by Federal Law No. 185-ФЗ, 28 December 2002].

Article 2. Basic Terms Used in Present Federal Law

Emission security: any security, including paperless,
which is characterized simultaneously by the following indicia:
    – consolidates the aggregate of property and nonproperty
rights subject to certification, assignment, and unconditional
effectuation in compliance with the forms and procedure established by the present Federal Law;
    – is placed by issues;

– has an equal amount and periods for the effectuation of rights within a single issue irrespective of the time of acquisition of the security.

Stock: emission security consolidating the rights of its possessor (stockholder) to receive part of the profit of a joint-stock society in the form of dividends, to participation in the management of the joint-stock society, and to part of the property remaining after the liquidation thereof. A stock shall be an inscribed security [as amended by Federal Law No. 185-ФЗ, 28 December 2002].

Bond: an emission security consolidating the right of the possessor thereof to receive from the emitent of the bond within the period provided for by it the par value or other property equivalent. A bond may also provide for the right of the possessor thereof to receive interest fixed therein on the par value of the bond or other property rights. Interest and/or a discount shall be revenue with regard to the bond [as amended by Federal Law No. 185-ФЗ, 28 December 2002].

Option of emitent: an emission security consolidating the right of the possessor to purchase within the period provided therein and/or in the event of the ensuing of circumstances specified therein of a determined quantity of stocks of the emitent of such option at the price determined in the option of the emitent. An option of an emitent shall be an inscribed security. The adoption of the decision concerning the placement of options of an emitent and the placement thereof shall be effectuated in accordance with the rules established by federal laws for the placement of securities convertible into stocks. In so doing the price of the placement of stocks in performance of the requirements with regard to options of an emitent shall be determined in accordance with the price determined in such option [added by Federal Law No. 185-ФЗ, 28 December 2002].

Issue of emission securities: aggregate of all securities of one emitent granting an identical volume of rights to possessors thereof and having identical par value in instances when the presence of par value has been provided by legislation of the Russian Federation. A single State registration number which shall extend to all securities of the particular issue shall be conferred on an issue of emission securities [as amended by Federal Law No. 185-ФЗ, 28 December 2002].

Additional issue of emission securities: aggregate of securities placed additionally to the securities previously placed of the same issue of emission securities. Securities of an additional issue shall be placed on identical conditions [added by Federal Law No. 185-ФЗ, 28 December 2002].

Emitent: juridical person or agencies of executive power or agencies of local self-government bearing in its name obligations to possessors of securities with regard to the effectuation of the rights consolidated by them.

Inscribed emission securities: securities, information concerning the possessors of which must be accessible to the emitent in the form of a register of possessors of securities, the transfer of the rights to which and the effectuation of the rights consolidated by them requires obligatory identification of the possessor.

Emission bearer securities: securities, the transfer of the rights to which and the effectuation of the rights consolidated by them shall not require identification of the possessor.

Documentary form of emission securities: form of emission securities under which the possessor is established on the basis of the presentation of a duly formalized certificate of the security or, in the event of the deposit of such, on the basis of an entry relating to the deposit account.

Paperless form of emission securities: form of emission securities under which the possessor is established on the basis of an entry in the system of keeping the register of possessors of securities or, in the event of the deposit of securities, on the basis of an entry relating to the deposit account.

Decision concerning issue of securities: document containing data sufficient to establish the volume of rights consolidated by the security [as amended by Federal Law No. 185-ФЗ, 28 December 2002].

Certificate of emission security: document to be issued by emitent and certifying the aggregate of rights to the quantity of securities specified in the certificate. The possessor of securities shall have the right to demand from the emitent the performance of its obligations on the basis of such certificate.

Possessor: person to whom securities belong by right of ownership or other right to a thing.

Circulation of securities: conclusion of civil-law transactions entailing the transfer of the rights of ownership to securities.

Placement of emission securities: alienation of emission securities by emitent to primary possessors by means of conclusion of civil-law transactions.

Emission of securities: sequence of actions of emitent established by present Federal Law with regard to placement of emission securities.

Professional participants of securities market: juridical persons which effectuate the types of activity specified in Chapter 2 of the present Federal Law [as amended by Federal Law No. 185-ФЗ, 28 December 2002].

Financial consultant on securities market: juridical person having a license for the effectuation of broker and/or dealer activity on the securities market rendering services to an emitent with regard to the preparation of a securities prospectus [added by Federal Law No. 185-ФЗ, 28 December 2002].

Good-faith acquirer: person who has acquired securities, paid them up, and at the moment of acquisition did not know and could not know abut the rights of third persons to such securities, unless it is proved otherwise.

State registration number: figure (or letter, symbolic) code which identifies a specific issue of emission securities.

Public placement of securities: placement of securities

by means of an open subscription, including the placement of securities for public sale of stock exchanges and/or other organizers of trade on the securities market [added by Federal Law No. 185-ФЗ, 28 December 2002].

Public circulation of securities: circulation of securities for public sale of stock exchanges and/or other organizers of trade on the securities market and circulation of securities by means of proposing securities to an indeterminate group of persons, including with the use of advertisement [added by Federal Law No. 185-ФЗ, 28 December 2002].

Listing: inclusion of securities on a quoted list [added by Federal Law No. 185-ФЗ, 28 December 2002].

Delisting: exclusion of securities from a quoted list [added by Federal Law No. 185-ФЗ, 28 December 2002].

Section II. Professional Participants of Securities Market

Chapter 2. Types of Professional Activity on Securities Market

Article 3. Broker Activity

1. Activity with regard to the conclusion of civil-law securities transactions in the name of and at the expense of a client (including the emitent of emission securities in the event of the placement thereof) or in one's own name and at the expense of a client on the basic of compensated contracts with a client, shall be deemed to be broker activity [as amended by Federal Law No. 185-ФЗ, 28 December 2002].

A professional participant of the securities market effectuating broker activity shall be named a broker [as amended by Federal Law No. 185-ФЗ, 28 December 2002].

In the event of the rendering of services by a broker with

regard to the placement of emission securities, the broker shall have the right to acquire at his own expense securities not placed within the period provided for by the contract [added by Federal Law No. 185-ФЗ, 28 December 2002].

2. A broker must fulfil the commissions of clients in good faith and in the order of receiving them. Transactions to be effectuated on behalf of clients shall in all instances be subject to priority execution in comparison with dealer operations of the broker himself when he combines the activity of broker and dealer [as amended by Federal Law No. 185-ФЗ, 28 December 2002].

If a conflict of interests of a broker and his client, of which the client was not informed before receipt by the broker of the respective commission led to causing losses to the client, the broker shall be obliged to compensate them in the procedure established by civil legislation of the Russian Federation [as amended by Federal Law No. 185-ФЗ, 28 December 2002].

3. Monetary means of clients transferred by them to a broker for investing in securities, and also monetary means received under transactions concluded by the broker on the basis of contracts with clients, must be in a separate bank account(s) opened by the broker in a credit organisation (special broker account). A broker shall be obliged to keep a record of the monetary means of each client in a special broker account(s) and shall be accountable to the client. Execution may not be levied for obligations of the broker against monetary means of clients in a special broker account(s). A broker shall not have the right to deposit own monetary means in a special broker account(s), except for instances of the return thereof to a client and/or provision of a loan to a client in the procedure established by the present Article [added by Federal Law No. 185-ФЗ, 28 December 2002].

A broker shall have the right to use monetary means in his interests which are in a special broker account(s) if this has been provided for by a contract concerning broker servicing, guaranteeing to the client the execution of his commissions at the expense of the said monetary means or the return thereof at the demand of the client. Monetary means of clients who have granted the right to the use thereof to a broker in his interests must be in a special broker account(s) separate from the special broker account(s) in which the monetary means of clients are situated who have not granted such right to the broker. Monetary means of clients who have granted to a broker the right to the use thereof may be credited by the broker to his own bank account [added by Federal Law No. 185-ФЗ, 28 December 2002].

The requirements of the present point shall not extend to credit organisations [added by Federal Law No. 185-ФЗ, 28 December 2002].

4. A broker shall have the right to provide a loan of monetary means to a client and/or securities for the conclusion of purchase-sale securities transactions on condition of the provision by the client of security by the means provided for by the present point. Transactions concluded with the use of monetary means and/or securities transferred by a broker on loan shall be called margin transactions [added by Federal Law No. 185-ФЗ, 28 December 2002].

The conditions of a contract of loan, including the amount of the loan or procedure for determination thereof, may be determined by a contract on broker servicing. In so doing the document certifying the transfer of a determined monetary amount on loan or determined quantity of securities shall be deemed to be the report of the broker concerning margin transactions concluded or another document determined by the conditions of the contract [added by Federal Law No. 185-ФЗ, 28 December 2002].

A broker shall have the right to recover interest from a client for the loans provided. A broker shall have the right to accept as security for obligations of a client with regard to loans provided only securities belonging to the client and/or acquired by the broker for the client under margin transactions [added by Federal Law No. 185-ФЗ, 28 December 2002].

The amount of security provided by a client shall be determined by the broker at the market cost of securities acting as security which has formed in public sales of a stock exchange and/or other organizers of trade on the securities market, deducting the discount established by the contract. Securities acting as security for the obligations of a client with regard to loans provided by a broker shall be subject to revaluation [added by Federal Law No. 185-ФЗ, 28 December 2002].

In instances of the failure to return the amount of the loan and/or securities engaged within the period, the failure to pay interest within the period under the loan provided, and also if the amount of security becomes less than the amount of loan provided to the client (market value of securities engaged which has formed in public sales of a stock exchange, and/or other organisers of trade on the securities market), the broker shall levy execution against monetary means and/or securities acting as security of obligations of the client for loans provided by the broker in an extrajudicial procedure by means of the realisation of such securities in public sales of a stock exchange and/or other organisers of trade on the securities market [added by Federal Law No. 185-ФЗ, 28 December 2002].

Only liquid securities included in a quoted list of organisers of trade on the securities market may be accepted as security for obligations of a client with regard to loans provided by a broker. The criteria of liquidity of the said securities accepted by a broker as security and the procedure and conditions of revaluation thereof, and also requirements for periods and the procedure and conditions of the realisation of securities acting as security for the obligations of a client with regard to loans provided by a broker, shall be established by normative legal acts of the federal agency of executive power for securities [added by Federal Law No. 185-ФЗ,

28 December 2002].

Article 4. Dealer Activity

The conclusion of purchase-sale securities transactions in his own name and for his own account by means of the public announcement of the prices of purchase and/or sale of determined securities with the obligation of purchase and/or sale of these securities at the prices declared by the person effectuating such activity shall be deemed to be dealer activity.

A professional participant of the securities market effectuating dealer activity shall be named a dealer. Only a juridical person which is a commercial organization may be a dealer.

Besides prices, a dealer shall have the right to announce other material conditions of the contract of purchase-sale of securities: the minimum and maximum quantity of securities to be purchased and/or sold, and also the period during which the announced prices operate. In the absence in the announcement of an indication of other material conditions the dealer shall be obliged to conclude a contract on the material conditions offered by his client. In the event the dealer evades the conclusion of the contract, a suit may be brought against him concerning the compulsory conclusion of such contract and/or compensation of the losses caused to the client.

Article 5. Activity Relating to Management of Securities

For the purpose of the present Federal Law activity relating to the management of securities shall be deemed to be the effectuation by a juridical person in its own name for remuneration during a determined period which are transferred to it in possession and which belong to another person in the interests of this person or of third persons specified by this person the trust management of [as amended by Federal Law No. 185-ФЗ, 28 December 2002]:

– securities;

– monetary means intended for investing in securities;

– monetary means and securities received in the process of management of the securities.

A professional participant of the securities market effectuating activity relating to the management of securities shall be named a manager.

The presence of a license for the effectuation of activity relating to the management of securities shall not be required if trust management is connected only with the management of rights with regard to securities [added by Federal Law No. 185-ФЗ, 28 December 2002];

The procedure for the effectuation of activity relating to the management of securities and the rights and duties of the manager shall be determined by legislation of the Russian Federation and by contracts.

The manager when effectuating his activity shall be obliged to specify that he is acting as a manager.

If a conflict of interests of the manager and his client or of various clients of one manager, of which all the parties were not informed beforehand, had led to actions of the manager which inflicted damage on the interests of the client, the manager shall be obliged on his own account to compensate the losses in the procedure established by civil legislation.

Article 6. Activity Relating to Determination of Mutual Obligations (Clearing)

Clearing activity is activity relating to the determination of mutual obligations (collection, verification, and adjustment of information relating to securities transactions and the preparation of bookkeeping documents regarding them) and the set-off thereof with regard to deliveries of securities and settlements of accounts regarding them.

Organisations effectuating clearing with regard to securities in connection with the settlement of accounts regarding securities operations shall accept for execution bookkeeping documents prepared when determining mutual obligations on the basis of their contracts with participants of the securities market for which the settlement of accounts is made.

A clearing organisation effectuating the settlement of accounts with regard to securities transactions shall be obliged to form special funds in order to reduce the risks of the failure to perform securities transactions. The minimum amount of special funds of clearing organisations shall be established by the federal agency of executive power for the securities market by agreement with the Central Bank of the Russian Federation [as amended by Federal Law No. 185-ФЗ, 28 December 2002].

A clearing organisation shall be obliged to confirm rules for the effectuation of clearing activity [added by Federal Law No. 185-ФЗ, 28 December 2002].

A clearing organisation shall be obliged to register the rules for the effectuation of clearing activity, and also changes in and additions thereto, at the federal agency of executive power for the securities market [added by Federal Law No. 185-ФЗ, 28 December 2002].

Article 7. Depositary Activity

The rendering of services relating to the keeping of securities certificates and/or the recording and transfer of the rights to securities shall be deemed to be depositary activity.

A professional participant of the securities market effectuating depositary activity shall be named a depositary. Only a juridical person may be a depositary.

A person enjoying the services of a depositary with regard to keeping securities and/or recording rights to securities shall be named the depositor.

A contract between the depositary and the depositor regulating their relations in the process of depositary activity shall be named a depositary contract (or contract on deposit account). The depositary contract must be concluded in written form. The depositary shall be obliged to confirm the conditions of the effectuation of depositary activity by him, which shall be an integral constituent part of the depositary contract concluded.

The conclusion of a depositary contract shall not entail the transfer to the depositary of the right of ownership to securities of the depositor. Depositaries shall not have the right to dispose of securities of the depositor, to manage them, or to effectuate in the name of the depositor any actions with securities except those to be effectuated on behalf of the depositor in instances provided for by the depositary contract. Depositaries shall not have the right to condition the conclusion of a depositary contract upon the waiver by the depositor of any one of the rights consolidated by the securities. Depositaries shall bear civil-law responsibility for the preservation of securities certificates deposited with them.

Execution may not be levied with regard to obligations of a depositary on securities of the depositors.

Depositaries shall have the right on the basis of agreements with other depositaries to involve them in the performance of their duties relating to keeping securities certificates and/or recording rights of depositors to securities (that is, to become the depositor of another depositary or to accept another depositary as depositor), unless this is expressly prohibited by the depositary contract.

If the depositor of one depositary is another depositary, then the deposit contract between them must provide for a procedure to receive information in the instances provided for by legislation of the Russian Federation concerning the possessors of securities, the recording of which is conducted in the depositary-depositor, and also in its depositaries-depositors.

The depositary contract must contain the following material conditions:

– an unequivocal determination of the subject of the contract: the granting of services relating to keeping securities certificates and/or recording the rights to securities;

– the procedure for the transfer by the depositor to the depositary of information concerning the disposition of securities of the depositor deposited in the depositary;

– the period of operation of the contract;

– the amount and procedure for paying for the services of the depositary provided by the contract;

– the form and periodicity of a report of the depositary to the depositor;

– the duties of the depositary.

There shall be within the duties of the depositary:

– the registration of facts of encumberment of securities of the depositor with obligations;

– the conducting of a deposit of the depositor separately from other account, specifying the date and grounds for each operation relating to the account;

– the transfer to the depositor of all information concerning the securities received by the depositary from the emitent or holder of the register of possessors of securities.

Depositaries shall have the right to be registered in the system of conducting the register of possessors of securities or with another depositary as a nominee holder in accordance with the depositary contract.

Depositaries shall bear responsibility for the failure to perform or the improper performance of its duties with regard to recording the rights to securities, including for the completeness and correctness of the entries relating to deposit accounts.

Depositaries shall in accordance with a depositary contract have the right to receive revenues in their account relating to securities which are being kept for the purpose of crediting to the accounts of depositors.

Article 8. Activity Relating to Conducting Register of Possessors of Securities

1. The collection, fixation, processing, keeping, and provision of data constituting the system of conducting the register of possessors of securities shall be deemed to be activity relating to the conducting of the register of possessors of securities.

Only juridical persons shall have the right to engage in activity relating to the conducting of the register of possessors of securities.

Persons effectuating activity relating to conducting the register of possessors of securities shall be called holders of the register (registrars).

A juridical person effectuating activity relating to conducting the register of possessors of securities shall not have the right to effectuate transactions with securities registered in the system of conducting the register of possessors of securities of an emitent.

The system of conducting the register of possessors of securities is understood to be the aggregate of data fixed on a paper bearer and/or with the use of electronic data bases ensuring the identification of nominee holders and possessors of securities registered in the system of conducting the register of possessors of securities and recording their rights with respect to securities registered in their name enabling them to receive and send information to the said persons and to compile the register of possessors of securities.

The system of conducting the register of possessors of securities must ensure the collection and keeping during the periods established by legislation of the Russian Federation of information concerning all facts and documents entailing the necessity to make changes in the system of conducting the register of possessors of securities and all actions of the holder of the register relating to making these changes.

A system for conducting the register of possessors of securities shall not be conducted for bearer securities.

The register of possessors of securities (hereinafter: register) is part of the system of conducting the register, representing a list of registered possessors with an indication of the quantity, par value, and categories of inscribed securities belonging to them drawn up as of any established date and enabling these possessors and the quantity and category of securities belonging to them to be identified.

The possessors and nominee holders of securities shall be obliged to comply with the rules for the submission of information to the system of conducting the register.

The holder of the register may be the emitent or professional participant of the securities market effectuating activity relating to conducting the register on the basis of a commission of the emitent. If the number of possessors exceeds 500, the holder of the register must be an independent specialized organisation which is a professional participant of the securities market and effectuating activity relating to conducting the register. The registrar shall have the right to delegate part of his functions with regard to the collection of information to be entered in the system for conducting the register to other registrars. The transfer of functions shall not relieve the registrar form responsibility to the emitent.

A contract for conducting the register shall be concluded only with one juridical person. The registrar may conduct the registers of possessors of securities of an unlimited number of emitents.

2. The nominee holder of securities is a person registered in the system of conducting the register, including the depositor of a depositary and who is not the possessor with respect

to these securities.

Professional participants of the securities market may act as nominee holders of securities. Depositaries may be registered as a nominee holder of securities in accordance with the depositary contract. A broker may be registered as a nominee holder of securities in accordance with the contract on the basis of which he services a client.

A nominee holder of securities may effectuate the rights consolidated by the security only in the event of receiving the respective power from the possessor.

Data concerning a nominee holder of securities shall be subject to entry in the system of conducting the register by the holder of the register on behalf of the possessor or nominee holder of securities if the last persons have been registered in this system for conducting the register.

The entry of the name of a nominee holder of securities in the system of conducting the register, and also the re-registration of securities in the name of a nominee holder, shall not entail the transfer of the right of ownership and/or other right to a thing to securities to the last. Securities of clients of a nominee holder of securities shall not be subject to levy to the benefit of creditors of the last.

Securities operations between the possessors of securities of one nominee holder of securities shall not be reflected with the holder of the register or depositary of which he is a client.

The nominee holder with respect to inscribed securities of which he is the holder shall be obliged in the interests of the other person to:

– perform all necessary actions directed towards ensuring the receipt by this person of all payments which are due to him with regard to these securities;

– effectuate transactions and securities operations exclusively on behalf of the person in whose interests he is a nominee holder of securities and in accordance with the contract concluded with this person;

– effectuate the recording of securities which he holds in the interests of other persons on separate balanced accounts and permanently has in separate balanced accounts a sufficient quantity of securities for the purpose of satisfying the demands of persons in whose interests he holds these securities.

A nominee holder of securities shall at the demand of the possessor be obliged to ensure the making of an entry in the system of conducting the register concerning the transfer of securities in the name of the possessor.

In order for possessors to effectuate the rights consolidated by securities the holder of a register shall have the right to demand from the nominee holder of the securities the granting of a list of possessors for whom he is a nominee holder as of a determined date. The nominee holder of securities shall be obliged to draw up the list demanded and to send it to the holder of the register within seven days after receipt of the demand. If the list demanded is necessary in order to draw up the register, then the nominee holder of securities shall not receive remuneration for drawing up this list.

The nominee holder of securities shall bear responsibility for the refusal to grant the said lists to the holder of the register to his clients, the holder of the register and the emitent in accordance with legislation of the Russian Federation.

3. The emitent who has charged the conducting the system for conducting the register to the registrar may once a year demand from the last the granting of the register for remuneration not exceeding the expenditures for the drawing up thereof, and the registrar shall be obliged to grant the register for such remuneration. In remaining instances the amount of remuneration shall be determined by the contract of the emitent and the registrar.

The holder of the register shall have the right to recover payment from the parties to a transaction corresponding to the quantity of dispositions concerning the transfer of securities and identical for all juridical and natural persons. The holder of the register shall not have the right to recover payment from the parties to a transaction in the form of interest on the volume of the transaction.

The procedure for determining the maximum amount of payment for services of the holder of the register with regard to inserting data in the register and issuing extracts from the register shall be determined by the federal agency of executive power for the securities market [as amended by Federal Law No. 185-ФЗ, 28 December 2002].

A suit concerning compensation for damage (including lost advantage) which arose from the impossibility to effectuate the rights consolidated by securities may be brought against the person who permitted the improper performance of the procedure for maintenance of the system of conducting and drawing up the register and a violation of the forms of report (against the emitent, registrar, depositary, possessor).

The holder of the register shall be obliged upon the demand of the possessor or of the person acting in his name, and also the nominee holder of securities, to grant an extract from the system of conducting the register with regard to his personal account within five work days. The possessor of securities shall not have the right to demand inclusion in the extract from the system of conducting the register information not relevant to him, including information concerning other possessors of securities and the quantity of securities belonging to them.

A document issued by the holder of the register specifying the possessor of the personal account, quantity of securities of each issue included in this account at the moment of the issuance of the extract, facts of the encumberment thereof by obligations, and also other information relevant to these securities, shall be an extract from the system of conducting the register.

An extract from the system of conducting the register must contain a notation concerning all limitations or facts of encumberment with obligations of securities for which the extract is issued fixed on the date of drawing up in the system of conducting the register.

Extracts from the system of conducting the register formalized when placing securities shall be issued to possessors free of charge.

The person who issued the said extract shall bear responsibility for the completeness and reliability of the information contained therein.

The rights and duties of the holder of the register, the procedure for the effectuation of activity with regard to conducting the register shall be determined by prevailing legislation and by the contract concluded between the registrar and the emitent.

There shall be within the duties of the holder of the register:

– to open for each possessor expressing the wish to be registered with the holder of the register, and also for the nominee holder of securities, a personal account in the system of conducting the register on the basis of notification concerning the assignment of a demand or instruction concerning the transfer of securities, and when placing emission securities, on the basis of a notification of the seller of the securities;

– insert in the system of conducting the register all necessary changes and additions;

– perform operations in personal accounts of possessors and nominee holders of securities only on their behalf;

– bring to registered persons information granted by the emitent;

– grant to possessors and nominee holders of securities registered in the system of conducting the register who possess more than 1% of the voting stocks of the emitent data from the register concerning the names of the possessors registered in the register and the quantity, categories, and par value of the securities belonging to them;

– inform the possessors and nominee holders of securities registered in the system of conducting the register about the rights consolidated by the securities and on the means and procedure for effectuating these rights;

– strictly comply with the procedure for the transfer of the system of conducting the register when dissolving the contract with the emitent.

The form of instruction concerning the transfer of securities and information specified therein shall be established by the federal agency of executive power for the securities market [as amended by Federal Law No. 185-ФЗ, 28 December 2002].

The holder of the register shall not have the right to present additional requirements when making changes in the data of the system of conducting the register except those which are established in the procedure provided for by the present Federal Law.

In the event of the termination of the operation of the contract for the maintenance of the system of conducting the register between the emitent and the registrar, the last shall transfer to another holder of the register for the said emitent the information received from the emitent, all data and documents comprising the system of conducting the register, and also the register drawn up on the date of termination of the operation of the contract. The transfer shall be made on the day of dissolution of the contract.

In the event of the replacement of the holder of the register, the emitent shall make an announcement thereof in the mass media or inform all possessors of the securities in writing at its expense.

All extracts issued by the holder of the register after the date of termination of the contract with the emitent shall be invalid.

The holder of the register shall make changes in the system of conducting the register on the basis of:

– an instruction of the possessor concerning the transfer of securities or the person acting in his name, or the nominee holder of securities who is registered in the system of conducting the register in accordance with the rules for conducting the register established by legislation of the Russian Federation, and when placing emission securities, in accordance with the procedure established by the present Article;

– other documents confirming the transfer of the right of ownership to securities in accordance with civil legislation of the Russian Federation.

In the event of the documentary form of emission securities providing for the securities to be situated with the possessors thereof, in addition to the said documents the certificate of the security also shall be submitted. In so doing the name of the person specified in the certificate as the possessor of the inscribed security must correspond to the name of the registered person specified in the instruction concerning the transfer of securities.

A refusal to make an entry in the system of conducting the register or the evasion of such entry, including with respect to a good faith acquirer, shall not be permitted except for the instances provided for by Federal laws.

Article 9. Activity Relating to Organisation of Trade on Securities Market

The provision of services directly facilitating the conclusion of civil-law securities transactions between participants of the securities market shall be deemed to be activity relating to organisation of trade on the securities market.

A professional participant of the securities market effectuating activity relating to the organisation of trade on the securities market shall be called the organiser of trade on the securities market.

The organiser of trade on the securities market shall be obliged to disclose the following information to any interested person:

the rules for admitting a participant of the securities market to public sales;

the rules for admittance to public sales of securities;

the rules for the conclusion and verification of transactions;

the rules for the registration of transactions;

the procedure for the performance of transactions;

the rules limiting the manipulation of prices;

the schedule for granting of services by the organiser of trade on the securities market;

the reglament for making changes in and additions to the aforesaid provisions;

the list of securities permitted for public sale.

The following information shall be granted to any interested person concerning each transaction concluded in accordance with the rules established by the organiser of trade:

the date and time of conclusion of a transaction;

the name of the securities which are the subject of the transaction;

the State registration number of the securities;

the price of a single security;

the quantity of securities.

An organiser of trade on the securities market shall be obliged to register at the federal agency of executive power for the securities market documents containing information specified in paragraph three of the present Article, and also changes in and additions thereto [added by Federal Law No. 185-ФЗ, 28 December 2002].

Article 10. Combining of Professional Types of Activity on Securities Market

The effectuation of activity with regard to keeping the register shall not permit the combining thereof with other types of professional activity on the securities market.

Limitations on the combining of types of activity and securities operations shall be established by the federal agency of executive power for the securities market [as amended by Federal Law No. 185-ФЗ, 28 December 2002].

Article 10¹. Requirements for Officials of Professional Participants of Securities Market

1. The functions of a one-man executive organ of a professional participant of the securities market may not be effectuated by:

persons who have effectuated the function of one-man executive organ or entered the composition of a collegial executive organ of a management company of joint-stock investment funds, share investment funds, and non-State pension funds, specialized depositary of joint-stock investment funds, share investment funds, and non-State pension funds, joint-stock investment fund, professional participant of the securities market, credit organisation, insurance organisation, and non-State pension fund at the moment of the annulment (or revocation) of licenses of those organisations for the effectuation of the respective types of activity for a violation of licensing requirements or at the moment of rendering of a decision concerning the application of procedures of bankruptcy, if at the moment of such annulment or moment of completion of the procedures of bankruptcy less than three years have elapsed;

persons having a record of conviction for a crime in the sphere of economic activity or crime against State power.

The said persons also may not be within the composition of the council of directors (or supervisory council) and collegial executive organ of a professional participant of the securities market, and also effectuate the functions of an executive of a control subdivision (or controller) of a professional participant of the securities market.

2. The federal agency of executive power for the securities market must be informed about the person elected to the office of one-man executive organ and about the person appointed as executive of the control subdivision (or controller) of a stock exchange and professional participant of the securities market effectuating clearing activity and depositary effectuating settlements of accounts with regard to the results of transactions concluded in public sales of stock exchanges and/or other organisers of trade on the securities market by agreement with such stock exchanges and/or organisers of trade (or settlement depositary) [Article added by Federal Law No. 185-ФЗ, 28 December 2002].

Chapter 3. Stock Market

Article 11. Stock Exchange [as amended by Federal Law No. 185-ФЗ, 28 December 2002]

1. An organiser of trade on the securities market which meets the requirements established by the present Chapter shall be deemed to be a stock exchange [as amended by Federal Law No. 185-ФЗ, 28 December 2002].

2. A juridical person may effectuate the activity of a stock exchange if it is a noncommercial partnership or joint-stock society [as amended by Federal Law No. 185-ФЗ, 28 December 2002].

3. To one stockholder of a stock exchange and affiliated persons thereof may not belong 20% or more of the stocks of

each category (or type), and to one member of a stock exchange of a noncommercial partnership may not belong 20% or more of the votes at a general meeting of the members of such exchange.

The limitations specified in paragraph one of the present point shall not apply to stockholders (or members) of a stock exchange which are stock exchanges.

Only professional participants of the securities market may be members of a stock exchange which is a noncommercial partnership. In so doing the procedure for joining such a stock exchange, and the withdrawal and expulsion of members of a stock exchange, shall be determined by such stock exchange autonomously on the basis of its internal documents [as amended by Federal Law No. 185-ФЗ, 28 December 2002].

4. A juridical person effectuating the activity of a stock exchange shall not have the right to combine the said activity with other types of activity, except for activity of a currency exchange, goods exchange (or activity with regard to the organisation of exchange trade), clearing activity connected with the effectuation of clearing with regard to securities operations and investment shares of share investment funds, activity with regard to the dissemination of information, publishing activity, and also the effectuation of activity with regard to leasing out property.

In the event of the combining by a juridical person of activity of a currency exchange and/or goods exchange (or activity with regard to the organisation of exchange trade), and/or with the activity of a stock exchange, for the effectuation of each of the said types of activity an individual structural subdivision must be created [as amended by Federal Law No. 185-ФЗ, 28 December 2002].

5. A person effectuating the functions of one-man executive organ, executive of a control subdivision (or controller) of a stock exchange, and other workers of a stock exchange may not be workers and/or participants of professional

participants of the stock market who are participants of public sales for the particular and/or other stock exchanges [as amended by Federal Law No. 185-ФЗ, 28 December 2002].

6. Stock exchanges which are noncommercial partnerships may be transformed into joint-stock societies. A decision concerning such transformation shall be adopted by members of such stock exchange by a majority of three-quarters of the votes of all members of this stock exchange [as amended by Federal Law No. 185-ФЗ, 28 December 2002].

Article 12. Participants of Public Sales on Stock Exchange [as amended by Federal Law No. 185-ФЗ, 28 December 2002]

Only brokers, dealers, and managers may be participants in public sales on a stock exchange.

Participants in public sales on a stock exchange created in the form of a noncommercial partnership may be only members of such an exchange.

The procedure for admission to participate in public sales and expel from among the participants of public sales shall be determined by the rules established by the stock exchange.

An unequal status of participants in public sales on a stock exchange, and also the transfer of the right to participate in public sales on a stock exchange to third persons, shall not be permitted [as amended by Federal Law No. 185-ФЗ, 28 December 2002].

Article 13. Requirements for Activity of Stock Exchange

1. A stock exchange shall be obliged to confirm:

the rules for admission to participate in public sales on the stock exchange;

the rules for conducting public sales on a stock exchange

which must contain rules for the conclusion and registration of transactions, measures directed towards prevention of the manipulation of prices and use of employment information.

A stock exchange rendering services directly facilitating the conclusion of securities transactions, including with investment shares of share investment funds, also shall be obliged to confirm the rules of listing/delisting securities and/or rules for the admission of securities to public sales without undergoing the procedure of listing, and a stock exchange rendering services directly facilitating the conclusion of transactions, the performance of obligations under which depends upon changes of prices for securities or changes of the significance of indices calculated on the basis of aggregate prices for securities (stock exchange indices), including transactions providing for exclusively the duty of the parties to pay monetary amounts depending upon the change of prices for securities or changes of the significance of stock exchange indices, shall be obliged also to confirm the specifications of such transactions which conform to the requirements of normative legal acts of the federal agency of executive power for the securities market.

A stock exchange shall be obliged to register at the federal agency of executive power for the securities market documents specified in the present point, and also changes in and additions thereto [as amended by Federal Law No. 185-ФЗ, 28 December 2002].

2. A stock exchange must effectuate permanent control over transactions concluded on the stock exchange for the purpose of eliciting instances of the use of employment information, manipulation of prices, and compliance by participants of public sales and emitents whose securities are included on the quoted lists with requirements of legislation of the Russian Federation concerning securities and normative legal acts of the federal agency of executive power for the securities market.

The participants of public sales shall be obliged to provide to the stock exchange at its request information necessary for the effectuation of control by it in accordance with the rules for conducting public sales on the stock exchange [as amended by Federal Law No. 185-ФЗ, 28 December 2002].

3. A stock exchange shall be obliged to ensure glasnost and publicity of public sales being conducted by means of notification of participants in public sales about the place and time of conducting public sales, the list and quoting of securities admitted to public sales on the stock exchange, the results of trading sessions, and also provide other information specified in Article 9 of the present Federal Law [as amended by Federal Law No. 185-ФЗ, 28 December 2002].

4. A stock exchange shall have the right to establish the amount and procedure for levying contributions, charges, and other payments from participants in public sales for services rendered by it, and also the amount and procedure for the recovery of fines for a violation of the rules established by it.

A stock exchange shall not have the right to establish the amount of remuneration recovered by participants of public sales for the conclusion of stock-exchange transactions [as amended by Federal Law No. 185-ФЗ, 28 December 2002].

Article 14. Admittance of Securities to Public Sales on Stock Exchange [as amended by Federal Law No. 185-ФЗ, 28 December 2002]

Emission securities corresponding to the requirements of legislation of the Russian Federation may be admitted to public sales on a stock exchange in the process of their placement and circulation, and also other securities, including investment shares of share investment funds in the process of their issuance and circulation. Investment shares of share investment funds shall be admitted for issuance and circulation on a stock exchange in the instances and procedure which have been established by normative legal acts of the federal agency of executive power for the securities market.

The rules for listing/delisting of securities, including investment shares of share investment funds, must correspond to the requirements of normative legal acts of the federal agency of executive power for the securities market. The listing of emission securities shall be effectuated by a stock exchange on the basis of a contract with the emitent of securities, and the listing of investment shares of a share investment fund – on the basis of a contract with the management company of this share investment fund. Only securities which correspond to the requirements of legislation of the Russian Federation and normative legal acts of the federal agency of executive power for the securities market may be included in quotation lists. In so doing a stock exchange shall have the right to establish additional requirements for securities included in quotation lists.

Securities may be admitted to public sales on a stock exchange without undergoing the procedure of listing in accordance with the rules of the admittance of securities to public sales without undergoing the procedure of listing [as amended by Federal Law No. 185-ФЗ, 28 December 2002].

Article 15. Settlement of Disputes Arising in Connection with Effectuation of Trade in Securities on Stock Exchange

Disputes between participants in public sales on a stock exchange and participants in public sales on a stock exchange and their clients shall be considered by a court, arbitrazh court, or arbitration court [as amended by Federal Law No. 185-ФЗ, 28 December 2002].

Section III. On Emission Securities

Chapter 4. Basic Provisions on Emission Securities

Article 16. General Provisions

Emission securities may be inscribed or bearer. Inscribed emission securities may be issued only in paperless form, except for instances provided for by federal laws. Bearer emission securities may be issued only in documentary form [as amended by Federal Law No. 185-ФЗ, 28 December 2002].

A certificate shall be issued for each bearer emission security to the possessor thereof. Upon the demand of a possessor one certificate may be issued for two or more bearer emission securities of one issue acquired by him. The present provision shall not apply to bearer emission securities with obligatory centralised keeping [as amended by Federal Law No. 185-ФЗ, 28 December 2002].

A certificate of bearer emission securities must contain the requisites provided for by the present Federal Law. The requirements for blanks of certificates of bearer emission securities, except for blanks of certificates of bearer emission securities with obligatory centralised keeping, shall be established by normative legal acts of the Russian Federation [as amended by Federal Law No. 185-ФЗ, 28 December 2002].

The total quantity of bearer emission securities specified on all certificates issued by the emitent must not exceed the quantity of bearer emission securities in the particular issue [as amended by Federal Law No. 185-ФЗ, 28 December 2002].

By decision concerning the issue of bearer emission securities, and in the instances provided for by federal laws, by decision concerning the issue of inscribed emission securities, it may be determined that such securities are subject to obligatory keeping in a depositary determined by the emitent (emission securities with obligatory centralised keeping). A certificate of bearer emission securities with obligatory centralised keeping may not be issued by hand to the possessor(s) of such securities [as amended by Federal Law No. 185-ФЗ, 28 December 2002].

[paragraph six repealed by Federal Law No. 185-ФЗ, 28 December 2002]

[paragraph seven repealed by Federal Law No. 185-ФЗ, 28 December 2002]

[paragraph eight repealed by Federal Law No. 185-ФЗ, 28 December 2002]

[paragraph nine repealed by Federal Law No. 185-ФЗ, 28 December 2002]

[paragraph ten repealed by Federal Law No. 185-ФЗ, 28 December 2002]

[paragraph eleven repealed by Federal Law No. 185-ФЗ, 28 December 2002]

[paragraph twelve repealed by Federal Law No. 185-ФЗ, 28 December 2002]

Any property and nonproperty rights consolidated in documentary or paperless form, irrespective of the name thereof, shall be emission securities if the conditions of their arising and circulation correspond to the aggregate of indicia of an emission security specified in Article 2 of the present Federal Law.

[paragraph fourteen repealed by Federal Law No. 185-ФЗ, 28 December 2002]

Russian emitents shall have the right to place securities beyond the limits of the Russian Federation, including by means of placement in accordance with foreign law of securities of foreign emitents certifying rights with respect to emission securities of Russian emitents, only upon the authorisation of the federal agency of executive power for the securities market [paragraph seven instead of fifteen by Federal Law No. 185-ФЗ, 28 December 2002].

Organisation of the circulation of emission securities of

a Russian emitent beyond the limits of the Russian Federation on the basis of a contract with the Russian emitent, including by means of placement in accordance with foreign law of securities of foreign emitents certifying rights with respect to emission securities of Russian emitents, shall be permitted only upon the authorisation of the federal agency of executive power for the securities market [paragraph eight added by Federal Law No. 185-ФЗ, 28 December 2002].

The said authorisations shall be issued by the federal agency of executive power for the securities market in compliance with the following conditions:

if the State registration of the issue (or additional issue) of securities of the Russian emitent has been effectuated;

if the securities of the Russian emitent have been included in the quotation list by at least one organiser of trade on the securities market;

if the quantity of securities of the Russian emitent whose placement or circulation is proposed beyond the limits of the Russian Federation, including by means of placement in accordance with foreign law of securities of foreign emitents certifying rights with respect to such securities, do not exceed normative standards established by normative legal acts of the federal agency of executive for the securities market;

if the contract on the basis of which the placement is effectuated in accordance with foreign law of securities of foreign emitents certifying rights with respect to stocks of Russian emitents provides that the right of vote with regard to the said stocks is effectuated not other than in accordance with the instructions of the possessors of the said securities of foreign emitents;

if other requirements established by federal laws have been complied with [paragraph nine added by Federal Law No. 185-ФЗ, 28 December 2002].

An authorisation for the placement and/or circulation of securities of Russian emitents beyond the limits of the Russian Federation shall be issued by the federal agency of executive power for the securities market on the basis of an application, to which shall be attached documents confirming compliance by the emitent with the requirements of the present Article. An exhaustive list of such documents shall be determined by normative legal acts of the federal agency of executive power for the securities market [paragraph ten added by Federal Law No. 185-ФЗ, 28 December 2002].

An authorisation for the placement of securities of Russian emitents beyond the limits of the Russian Federation may be issued simultaneously with the State registration of the issue (or additional issue) of such securities [paragraph eleven added by Federal Law No. 185-ФЗ, 28 December 2002].

The federal agency of executive power for the securities market shall be obliged to issue the said authorisation or adopt a reasoned decision concerning refusal of the issuance thereof within 30 days from the date of receipt of all necessary documents [paragraph twelve added by Federal Law No. 185-ФЗ, 28 December 2002].

The federal agency of executive power for the securities market shall have the right to conduct a verification of the reliability of the information contained in documents submitted for receipt of an authorisation. In this event the running of the period provided for by paragraph twelve of the present Article may be suspended for the time of conducting the verification, but not more than 30 days [paragraph thirteen added by Federal Law No. 185-ФЗ, 28 December 2002].

Article 17. Decision on Issue (or Additional Issue) of Emission Securities [as amended by Federal Law No. 185-ФЗ, 28 December 2002]

1. A decision concerning the issue (or additional issue) of emission securities must contain the following:
the full name of the emitent, location thereof, and postal

address;

the date of adoption of the decision concerning the place-ment of the emission securities;

the name of the empowered organ of the emitent which adopted the decision concerning placement of the emission securities;

the date of confirmation of the decision concerning the issue (or additional issue) of emission securities;

the name of the empowered organ of the emitent which confirmed the decision concerning the issue (or additional is-sue) of emission securities;

the type and category (or type) of emission securities;

the rights of the possessor consolidated by an emission security;

the conditions for the placement of emission securities;

an indication of the quantity of the emission securities in the particular issue (or additional issuance) of emission securi-ties;

an indication of the total quantity of emission securities in the particular issue previously placed (in the event of the placement of an additional issue of emission securities);

an indication of whether the emission securities are in-scribed or bearer;

the par value of the emission securities if the presence of a par value has been provided for by legislation of the Rus-sian Federation;

the signature of the person effectuating the functions of executive organ of the emitent and the seal of the emitent;

other information provided for by the present Federal Law or other federal laws on securities.

A description or sample of the certificate shall be ap-pended to the decision concerning the issue (or additional is-sue) of emission securities in documentary form [point 1 as amended by Federal Law No. 185-ФЗ, 28 December 2002].

2. The decision concerning the issue (or additional issue)

of emission securities of an economic society shall be confirmed by the council of directors (or supervisory council) or organ effectuating in accordance with federal laws the functions of the council of directors (or supervisory council) of this economic society. The decision concerning the issue (or additional issue) of emission securities of juridical persons of other organisational-legal forms shall be confirmed by the highest management organ unless established otherwise by federal laws.

The decision concerning the issue of bonds and the performance of the obligations with regard to which is secured by a pledge, bank guarantee, or other means provided for by the present Federal Law, also must contain information concerning the person who provided the security and the conditions of the security. The composition of information concerning the person providing the security shall be determined by the federal agency of executive power for the securities market. In this event the decision concerning the issue of bonds must also be signed by the person providing such security. A bond, performance of the obligations with regard to which is secured by one of the said means, also shall provide to the possessor thereof the right of demand against the person who provided such security.

The decision concerning the issue of inscribed bonds or documentary bonds with obligatory centralised keeping also must contain an indication of the date on which the list of possessors of bonds is drawn up for performance by the emitent of obligations with regard to the bonds. Such date may not be earlier than 14 days before the ensuing of the period of performance of the obligations with regard to the bonds. In so doing performance of an obligation with respect to a possessor included in the list of possessors of bonds shall be deemed to be proper, including in the event of the alienation of bonds after the date of drawing up the list of possessors of bonds [point 2 as amended by Federal Law No. 185-ФЗ, 28 December 2002].

3. An emitent shall not have the right to change a decision concerning the issue (or additional issue) of emission securities with respect to the amount of rights under the emission security established by this decision after the State registration of the issue (or additional issue) of emission securities [point 3 as amended by Federal Law No. 185-ФЗ, 28 December 2002].

4. The decision concerning the issue (or additional issue) of emission securities shall be drawn up in three examples. After State registration of an issue (or additional issue) of emission securities, one example of the decision concerning the issue of emission securities shall remain for keeping in the registering agency, and the two other examples shall be issued to the emitent. If the conducting of the register of possessors of inscribed emission securities of an emitent is effectuated by the registrar, and also if bearer emission securities placed by the emitent are emission securities with obligatory centralised keeping, one example of the decision concerning the issue of emission securities shall be transferred by the emitent for keeping to the registrar or depositary effectuating the obligatory centralised keeping. When there are divergencies in the texts of examples of a decision concerning the issue (or additional issue) of emission securities, the text of the document kept in the registering agency shall have preferential force [point 4 as amended by Federal Law No. 185-ФЗ, 28 December 2002].

5. In the event of the State registration of an issue (or additional issue) of emission securities a notation shall be made on each example of the decision concerning the issue (or additional issue) of emission securities concerning the State registration of the issue (or additional issue) of emission securities and the State registration number conferred on the issue (or additional issue) of emission securities shall be specified [point 5 as amended by Federal Law No. 185-ФЗ, 28 December

2002].

6. An emitent and/or registrar shall at the request of an interested person be obliged to provide him a copy of the decision concerning the issue (or additional issue) of emission securities for payment not exceeding the expenditures for the manufacture thereof [point 6 as amended by Federal Law No. 185-ФЗ, 28 December 2002].

Article 18. Form of Certification of Rights Comprising Emission Security

In the event of the documentary form of emission securities the certificate and decision concerning the issuance of securities shall be documents certifying the rights consolidated by the security.

In the event of the paperless form of emission securities the decision concerning the issuance of the securities shall be the document certifying the rights consolidated by the security.

An emission security shall consolidate property rights in that volume in which they have been established in the decision concerning the issuance of the particular securities and in accordance with legislation of the Russian Federation.

The certificate of an emission security must contain the following obligatory requisites:

full name of the emitent, location thereof, and postal address;

type and category (or type) of emission securities;

State registration number of issue of emission securities and date of State registration;

rights of possessor consolidated by emission security;

conditions of performance of obligations by person who provided security and information concerning this person in the event of the issue of bonds with security;

an indication of the quantity of emission securities certified by particular certificate;

an indication of the total quantity of emission securities in the particular issue of emission securities;

an indication of whether the emission securities are subject to obligatory centralised keeping, and if so subject – the name of the depositary effectuating the centralised keeping thereof;

an indication whether the emission securities are bearer emission securities;

signature of the person effectuating the functions of executive organ of the emitent and the seal of the emitent;

other requisites provided for by legislation of the Russian Federation for the particular type of emission securities [paragraph four as amended by Federal Law No. 185-ФЗ, 28 December 2002].

[paragraph five repealed by Federal Law No. 185-ФЗ, 28 December 2002]

In the event of a divergence between the text of the decision concerning the issuance of securities and data quoted in the certificate of an emission security, the possessor shall have the right to demand the effectuation of the rights consolidated by this security in the amount established by the certificate. The emitent shall bear responsibility for the failure of the data contained in the certificate of the emission security to coincide with the data contained in the decision concerning the issuance of securities, in accordance with legislation of the Russian Federation.

[paragraph seven repealed by Federal Law No. 185-ФЗ, 28 December 2002]

Chapter 5. Emission of Securities

Article 19. Procedure for Emission and Stages Thereof

1. The procedure for the emission of emission securities,

unless provided otherwise by federal laws, shall include the following stages:

adoption of a decision concerning the placement of emission securities;

confirmation of the decision concerning the issue (or additional issue) of emission securities;

State registration of the issue (or additional issue) of emission securities;

the placement of emission securities;

State registration of the report concerning the results of the issue (or additional issue) of emission securities.

Emission securities whose issue (or additional issue) did not undergo State registration in accordance with the requirements of the present Federal Law shall not be subject to placement.

In the event of the founding of a joint-stock society or reorganisation of juridical persons effectuated in the form of a merger, division, separation, and transformation, the placement of emission securities shall be effectuated before State registration of the issue thereof, and State registration of the report concerning the results of the issue of emission securities shall be effectuated simultaneously with State registration of the issue of emission securities [point one as amended by Federal Law No. 185-ФЗ, 28 December 2002].

2. State registration of an issue (or additional issue) of emission securities shall be accompanied by registration of the prospectus thereof in the event of the placement of emission securities by means of open subscription or by means of closed subscription among a group of persons, the number of which exceeds 500.

If State registration of an issue (or additional issue) of emission securities is accompanied by registration of the prospectus of securities, each stage of the procedure for the emission of securities shall be accompanied by the divulgence of information [point two as amended by Federal Law No. 185-

ФЗ, 28 December 2002].

3. If State registration of an issue (or additional issue) of emission securities has not been accompanied by registration of the prospectus thereof, it may be registered subsequently. In so doing registration of the securities prospectus shall be effectuated by the registering agency within 30 days from the date of receipt of the securities prospectus and other documents necessary for the registration thereof [point three as amended by Federal Law No. 185-ФЗ, 28 December 2002].

4. The peculiarities of the procedure for the issue of bonds of the Bank of Russia shall be determined by the Government of the Russian Federation in accordance with legislation of the Russian Federation [point four as amended by Federal Law No. 185-ФЗ, 28 December 2002].

5. The procedure for emission of State and municipal securities, and also the conditions of their placement, shall be regulated by federal laws or in the procedure established by federal laws [point five as amended by Federal Law No. 185-ФЗ, 28 December 2002].

Article 20. State Registration of Issues (or Additional Issues) of Emission Securities [as amended by Federal Law No. 185-ФЗ, 28 December 2002]

1. State registration of issues (or additional issues) of emission securities shall be effectuated by the federal agency of executive power for the securities market or other registering agency determined by a federal law (hereinafter – registering agency) [as amended by Federal Law No. 185-ФЗ, 28 December 2002].

2. State registration of an issue (or additional issue) of emission securities shall be effectuated on the basis of an application of the emitent.

To an application concerning State registration of an issue (or additional issue) of emission securities shall be appended the decision concerning the issue (or additional issue) of securities, documents confirming compliance by the emitent with the requirements of legislation of the Russian Federation determining the procedure and conditions of adoption of the decision concerning placement of securities, confirmation of the decision concerning the issue of securities, and other requirements, compliance with which is necessary when effectuating an emission of securities, and if registration of an issue (or additional issue) of securities in accordance with the present Federal Law must be accompanied by registration of a securities prospectus, the securities prospectus. An exhaustive list of such documents shall be determined by normative legal acts of the federal agency of executive power for the securities market [as amended by Federal Law No. 185-ФЗ, 28 December 2002].

3. The registering agency shall be obliged to effectuate State registration of an issue (or additional issue) of emission securities or to adopt a reasoned decision concerning a refusal of State registration of a issue (or additional issue) of emission securities within 30 days from the date of receipt of the documents submitted for State registration.

A registering agency shall have the right to conduct a verification of the reliability of information contained in documents submitted for State registration of an issue (or additional issue) of emission securities. In this event the running of the period provided for by paragraph one of the present point may be suspended for the time of conducting the verification, but not more than 30 days [as amended by Federal Law No. 185-ФЗ, 28 December 2002].

4. In the event of the State registration of an issue of emission securities an individual State registration number shall be conferred on it.

In the event of the State registration of each additional issue of emission securities an individual State registration number shall be conferred on it consisting of the individual

State registration number conferred on the issue of emission securities and the individual number (or code) of this additional issue of emission securities.

Upon the expiry of three months from the moment of State registration of the report concerning the results of an additional issue of emission securities, the individual number (or code) of the additional issue shall be annulled.

The procedure for conferment of the State registration numbers of issues of emission securities and annulment of individual numbers (or codes) of additional issues of emission securities shall be established by the federal agency of executive power for the securities market [as amended by Federal Law No. 185-ФЗ, 28 December 2002].

5. A registering agency shall be liable only for the fullness of information contained in documents submitted for State registration of the issue (or additional issue) of emission securities [as amended by Federal Law No. 185-ФЗ, 28 December 2002].

Article 21. Grounds for Refusal of Registration of Issue (or Additional Issue) of Emission Securities [as amended by Federal Law No. 185-ФЗ, 28 December 2002]

The grounds for the refusal of State registration of an issue (or additional issue) of emission securities and registration of a securities prospectus shall be [as amended by Federal Law No. 185-ФЗ, 28 December 2002]:

violation by the emitent of the requirements of legislation of the Russian Federation on securities, including the existence in the documents submitted of information enabling the conclusion to be drawn that the conditions of emission and circulation of emission securities are contrary to legislation of the Russian Federation and the nonconformity of the conditions of the issuance of emission securities to legislation of the Russian Federation on securities;

the failure of the documents submitted for State registration of an issue (or additional issue) of emission securities, or the registration of a securities prospectus, and the composition of information contained therein to conform to the requirements of the present Federal Law and normative legal acts of the federal agency of executive power for the securities market [as amended by Federal Law No. 185-ФЗ, 28 December 2002];

the failure to submit within 30 days at the request of the registering agency all documents necessary for State registration of an issue (or additional issue) of emission securities or registration of a securities prospectus [added by Federal Law No. 185-ФЗ, 28 December 2002];

the failure of a financial consultant on the securities market who signed the securities prospectus to conform to the established requirements [added by Federal Law No. 185-ФЗ, 28 December 2002];

the insertion in the securities prospectus or decision concerning the issue of securities (or other documents which are the grounds for registration of the issue of securities) of false information or information not corresponding to reality (unreliable information) [as amended by Federal Law No. 185-ФЗ, 28 December 2002].

The decision concerning a refusal of registration of the issue of securities and securities prospectus may be appealed to a court or arbitrazh court [as amended by Federal Law No. 185-ФЗ, 28 December 2002].

Article 22. General Requirements for Content of Securities Prospectus [as amended by Federal Law No. 185-ФЗ, 28 December 2002]

1. A securities prospectus must contain:

brief information concerning the persons within the composition of management organs of an emitent, information concerning bank accounts, auditor, valuer, and financial consultant of the emitent, and also other persons who have signed the prospectus;

brief information concerning the amount, periods, procedure, and conditions of the placement of emission securities;

basic information concerning the financial-economic state of the emitent and factors of risk;

detailed information concerning the emitent;

information concerning the financial-economic activity of the emitent;

detailed information concerning persons within the composition of the management organs of the emitent, organs of the emitent for control over its financial-economic activity and brief information concerning personnel (or workers) of the emitent;

information concerning participants (or stockholders) of the emitent and transactions concluded by the emitent in the conclusion of which there was an interest;

bookkeeping reports of the emitent and other financial information;

detailed information concerning the procedure and conditions for the placement of emission securities;

additional information concerning the emitent and placement by it of emission securities.

The requirements for information which must be specified on the title page of a securities prospectus shall be established by the standards for emission and securities prospectuses. A securities prospectus also must contain an introduction in which the basic information to be set out further in the securities prospectus is concisely set forth [as amended by Federal Law No. 185-ФЗ, 28 December 2002].

2. To the brief information concerning persons within the composition of management organs of the emitent, information concerning bank accounts, auditor, valuer, and financial consultant of the emitent, and also other persons who have

signed the prospectus, shall be relegated:

indication of the persons within the composition of management organs of the emitent;

information concerning bank accounts of the emitent, information concerning the auditor(s) of the emitent who have drawn up an opinion with respect to the yearly bookkeeping reports of the emitent for the last three completed financial years or for each completed financial year if the emitent effectuates its activity for less than three years;

information concerning the valuer and consultants of the emitent [as amended by Federal Law No. 185-ФЗ, 28 December 2002].

3. To brief information concerning the amount, periods, procedure, and conditions of the placement for each type or category (or type) of emission securities to be placed shall be relegated:

type or category (or type) and form of emission securities to be placed;

par value of each type or category (or type), and series of emission securities to be placed if the presence of par value has been provided for by legislation of the Russian Federation;

proposed size of the issue expressed in money and the quantity of emission securities which it is proposed to place;

price (or procedure for determining price) of placement of emission securities;

procedure and periods for placement of emission securities;

procedure and conditions of paying up emission securities to be placed;

procedure and conditions for conclusion of contracts in course of placement of emission securities;

group of potential acquirers of emission securities to be placed;

procedure for divulgence of information concerning

placement and results of placement of emission securities [as amended by Federal Law No. 185-ФЗ, 28 December 2002].

4. To basic information concerning financial-economic state of emitent shall be relegated information for the five last completed financial years or for each completed financial year if the emitent effectuates its activity for less than five years, and also for the last completed reporting period, including information concerning:

indicators of financial-economic activity of the emitent;

market capitalisation of the emitent and obligations thereof;

purposes of emission and orientations of the use of means received as a result of the placement of emission securities;

risks which arose in connection with the acquisition of emission securities to be placed [as amended by Federal Law No. 185-ФЗ, 28 December 2002].

5. To detailed information concerning the emitent shall be relegated information concerning:

the history of the creation and development of the emitent;

the basic economic activity of the emitent;

the plans for future activity of the emitent;

the participation of the eminent in industrial, banking, and financial groups, holding companies, concerns, and associations, and also subsidiary and dependent economic societies of the emitent;

the composition, structure, and value of basic means of the emitent, including plans with regard to the acquisition, replacement, and withdrawal of basic means, and also information concerning all facts of encumberment of basic means of the emitent [as amended by Federal Law No. 185-ФЗ, 28 December 2002].

6. To information concerning financial-economic activity of the emitent shall be relegated information concerning the financial state of the emitent and dynamics of the changes

thereof for the five last completed financial years or for each completed financial year if the emitent effectuates his activity for less than five years, and also an indication of the reasons and factors which, in the opinion of the management organs of the emitent, led to such changes, including concerning:

the results of financial-economic activity of the emitent, factors which have exerted an influence on a change of the amount of receipts from the sale by the emitent of goods, products, work, services, and profit (or losses) of the emitent from the basic activity, including the influence of inflation, change of exchange rates of foreign currencies, decisions of State agencies, other economic, financial, political, and other factors;

the liquidity of the emitent, amount, structure, and sufficiency of capital and circulating means of the emitent;

the policy and expenses of the emitent in the domain of scientific-technical development with respect to licenses and patents, new works, and research;

an analysis of the trends of development in the sphere of the basic activity of the emitent [as amended by Federal Law No. 185-ФЗ, 28 December 2002].

7. To detailed information concerning persons within the composition of management organs of the emitent, organs of the emitent for control over its financial-economic activity, and concise information concerning personnel (or workers) of the emitent shall be relegated:

information concerning persons within the composition of management organs of the emitent, including who are members of the council of directors (or supervisory council) of the emitent and members of the collegial executive management organ of the emitent, information concerning the person effectuating the functions of one-man executive management organ of the emitent (including information concerning a management organisation), information concerning persons effectuating the functions of internal auditor and/or members of the internal audit commission of the emitent, and also information concerning the character of any kinship links between any of the said persons;

information concerning the amount of remuneration, privileges, and/or contributory compensation of expenses for each management organ of the emitent (except for a natural person effectuating the functions of one-man executive organ) and organ of control over its financial-economic activity which has been paid by the emitent for the last completed financial year, and also information concerning existing agreements relative to such payment sin the current financial year;

information concerning the structure and competence of management organs of the emitent and organs of control over its financial-economic activity;

data concerning the number and summarised data concerning the formation and composition of personnel (or workers) of the emitent, and also changes of the number of personnel (or workers) of the emitent if such change is material for the emitent;

information concerning any obligations of the emitent to personnel (or workers) affecting the possibility of their participation in the charter (or contributed) capital (or share fund) of the emitent (or acquisition of stocks of the emitent), including any agreements which provide for the issue or provision of options of the emitent to personnel (or workers);

amount of participatory share of participation of persons specified in paragraph one of the present point in the charter (or contributed) capital (or share fund) of the emitent and its subsidiary and dependent societies, participatory shares belonging to the said persons of common stocks of the emitent and its subsidiary and dependent societies, and also information concerning options of the emitent and its subsidiary and dependent societies providing stocks of the emitent to such persons [as amended by Federal Law No. 185-ФЗ, 28 December 2002].

8. To information concerning participants (or stockhold-

ers) of the emitent and transactions concluded by the emitent in the conclusion of which there was an interest, shall be relegated:

information concerning the total quantity of participants (or stockholders) of the emitent;

information concerning the participants (or stockholders) of the emitent possessing not less than 5% of its charter (or contributed) capital (or share fund) or not less than 5% of its common stocks, including the amount of the participatory share of participant (or stockholder) of the emitent in its charter (or contributed) capital (or share fund), and also the participatory share of common stocks of the emitent belonging to it;

for participants (or stockholders) of the emitent possessing not less than 5% of its charter (or contributed) capital (or share fund) or not less than 5% of its common stocks, information concerning the participants (or stockholders) thereof possessing not less than 20% of the charter (or contributed) capital (or share fund) or not less than 20% of their common stocks, including an indication of their participatory share in the charter (or contributed) capital (or share fund) of the emitent, and also the participatory share belonging to them of the common stocks of the emitent;

information concerning the participatory share of participation of the State or municipal formation in the charter (or contributed) capital (or share fund) of the emitent and the presence of a special right ("golden stock");

information concerning limitations on participation in the charter (or contributed) capital (or share fund) of the emitent;

information concerning changes in the composition and amount of participation of participants (or stockholders) of the emitent possessing not less than 5% of its charter (or contributed) capital (or share fund) or not less than 5% of its common stocks for the five last completed financial years or for each completed financial year if the emitent effectuates its activity for less than five years;

information concerning the transactions concluded by the emitent, in the conclusion of which there was an interest, for the five last completed financial years or for each completed financial year if the emitent effectuates its activity for less than five years, and also for the period up to the date of confirmation of the securities prospectus;

information concerning the amount of debtor indebtedness for the five last completed financial years or for each completed financial year if the emitent effectuates its activity for less than five years, including a breakdown by debtors, the amount of indebtedness which comprises not less than 10% of the total amount of debtor indebtedness, and also information concerning debtor indebtedness to affiliated persons [as amended by Federal Law No. 185-ФЗ, 28 December 2002].

9. Bookkeeping reports of the emitent and other financial information shall be:

yearly bookkeeping reporting of the emitent for the three last completed financial years or for each completed financial year if the emitent effectuates its activity for less than three years, to which the opinion of an auditor(s) shall be appended with respect to the said bookkeeping reporting;

quarterly bookkeeping reporting of the emitent for the last completed reporting quarter;

composite bookkeeping reporting of the emitent for the three last completed financial years or for each completed financial year;

information concerning the total amount of export, and also the participatory share which export comprises in the total volume of sales;

information concerning material changes which have occurred in the composition of property of the emitent after the date of the end of the last completed financial year;

information concerning participation of the emitent in

judicial proceedings if such participation may materially reflect on the financial-economic activity of the emitent [as amended by Federal Law No. 185-ФЗ, 28 December 2002].

10. To detailed information concerning the procedure and conditions for placement of emission securities shall be relegated information concerning:

emission securities to be placed, price of the placement (or procedure for determining it), presence of preferential or other rights for the acquisition of emission securities to be placed, any limitations on the acquisition and circulation of emission securities to be placed;

dynamics of the change of prices for emission securities of the emitent if such securities were admitted to circulation by an organiser of trade on the securities market, including a stock exchange;

persons rendering services with regard to organisation of the placement and/or placement of the emission securities;

group of potential acquirers of emission securities;

organisers of trade on the securities market, including stock exchanges, on which the placement and/or circulation of the emission securities to be placed is proposed;

possible changes of the participatory share of participation of stockholders in the charter capital of the emitent as a result of the placement of emission securities;

expenses connected with the emission of securities;

means and procedure for the return of means received in payment of emission securities to be placed in the event of the issue (or additional issue) of emission securities being deemed to be unconstituted or invalid, and also in other instances provided for by legislation of the Russian Federation [as amended by Federal Law No. 185-ФЗ, 28 December 2002].

11. To additional information concerning an emitent and emission securities to be placed by it shall be relegated:

information concerning the amount, structure of the charter (or contributed) capital (or share fund) of the emitent and changes thereof for the five last completed financial years or for each completed financial year if the emitent effectuates its activity for less than five years, indicating the decision of empowered management organs of the emitent which are the basis for such changes;

information concerning each category (or type) of stocks of the emitent, indicating the rights granted by stocks to the possessors thereof, par value of each stock, quantity of stocks in circulation, quantity of additional stocks in the process of placement, quantity of declared stocks, quantity of stocks on the balance sheet of the emitent, quantity of additional stocks which may be placed as a result of converting placed emission securities convertible into stocks, or as a result of performance of obligations with regard to options of the emitent;

information concerning preceding issues of emission securities of the emitent, except for stocks of the emitent;

information concerning the structure of management organs of the emitent and their competence, and also the structure of organs of the emitent for control over its financial-economic activity and the competence thereof;

information concerning the procedure for the convocation and conducting of a meeting (or session) of the highest management organ of the emitent;

information concerning material transactions concluded by the emitent for the five last completed financial years or for each completed financial year if the emitent effectuates its activity for less than five years, the amount of obligations under which comprise not less than 10% of the balance sheet value of assets of the emitent according to data of its bookkeeping reporting for the last completed reporting period;

information concerning legislative acts regulating questions of the import and export of capital which may influence the payment of dividends, interest, and other payments to non-residents;

description of the procedure for the taxation of revenues

with regard to emission securities of the emitent placed and to be placed;

information concerning declared (or accumulated) and paid dividends with regard to stocks of the emitent, and also revenues with regard to bonds of the emitent for the five last completed financial years or for each completed financial year if the emitent effectuates its activity for less than five years, including the procedure for the payment of dividends and other revenues;

information concerning persons who provided security in the event of the issue of bonds with security by the emitent, and also the conditions for securing the performance of obligations with regard to bonds of the emitent;

information concerning credit ratings of the emitent, and also the change thereof for the five last completed financial years or for each completed financial year if the emitent effectuates its activity for less than five years;

information concerning commercial organisations in which the emitent possesses not less than 5% of the charter (or contributed) capital (or share fund) or not less than 5% of the common stocks;

information concerning the forming and use of the reserve fund, and also other funds of the emitent, for the last five completed financial years or for each completed financial year if the emitent effectuates its activity for less than five years;

information concerning organisations effectuating the recording of rights to emission securities of the emitent;

other information provided for by the present Federal Law or other federal laws [as amended by Federal Law No. 185-ФЗ, 28 December 2002].

12. The composition of information specified in points 2-11 of the present Article shall be determined by the federal agency of executive power for the securities market [as amended by Federal Law No. 185-ФЗ, 28 December 2002].

13. Unless established otherwise by the present Federal

Law or other federal laws, information contained in a securities prospectus shall indicate the date of its confirmation by the empowered management organ of the emitent [as amended by Federal Law No. 185-ФЗ, 28 December 2002].

14. If the registration of a securities prospectus is effectuated after the State registration of the issue of emission securities, the requirements of point 3 and point 10 (except for paragraph seven) of the present Article shall not apply [as amended by Federal Law No. 185-ФЗ, 28 December 2002].

Article 22¹. Confirmation and Signature of Securities Prospectus. Responsibility of Persons Who Have Signed Securities Prospectus [added by Federal Law No. 185-ФЗ, 28 December 2002]

1. A securities prospectus of an economic society shall be confirmed by the council of directors (or supervisory council) or organ effectuating in accordance with federal laws the functions of the council of directors (or supervisory council) of this economic society. The securities prospectus of juridical persons of other organisational-legal forms shall be confirmed by the person effectuating the functions of executive organ of the emitent unless established otherwise by federal laws.

2. A securities prospectus must be signed by the person effectuating the functions of one-man executive organ of the emitent, chief bookkeeper thereof (or other person fulfilling the functions thereof), thereby confirming the reliability and fullness of all information contained in the securities prospectus. A securities prospectus also must be signed by the auditor, and in instances provided for by normative legal acts of the federal agency of executive power for the securities market, an independent valuer, confirming the reliability of information in the part of the securities prospectus specified by them. In instances of a public placement and/or public circulation of emission securities the securities prospectus must be signed by

a financial consultant for the securities market, thereby confirming the reliability and fullness of all information contained in the securities prospectus, except for the part confirmed by the auditor and/or valuer. A financial consultant for the securities market may not be an affiliated person of the emitent.

The involvement of a financial consultant for the securities market when privatising stocks shall be effectuated in the instances and procedure which have been provided by legislation of the Russian Federation on privatisation.

In the event of the issue of bonds with security the person who has provided the security shall be obliged to sign the securities prospectus, thereby confirming the reliability of information concerning the security.

3. Persons who have signed the securities prospectus shall, in the event of their fault, bear jointly and severally between themselves subsidiary responsibility with the emitent for damage caused to the possessor of securities as a consequence of unreliable or incomplete information and/or information deluding an investor which was confirmed by them. In so doing the period of limitations for compensation of damage on the grounds specified in the present Article shall comprise three years from the day of commencement of the placement of the securities, and if State registration of the issue (or additional issue) of emission securities was not accompanied by the registration of the securities prospectus, from the day of commencement of public circulation of the emission securities.

Article 23. Information on Issue (or Additional Issue) of Emission Securities Disclosed by Emitent [as amended by Federal Law No. 185-ФЗ, 28 December 2002]

In the event of the registration of a securities prospectus, the emitent shall be obliged to ensure access to information contained in the securities prospectus to any persons interested in such irrespective of the purpose of receiving such information [as amended by Federal Law No. 185-Ф3, 28 December 2002].

In the event of an open subscription the emitent shall be obliged to publish a communication concerning State registration of the issue (or additional issue) of emission securities, in so doing having indicated the procedure for access of any interested persons to information contained in the securities prospectus, in a printed organ of the mass media distributed in a print-run of not less than 10,000 examples. In the event of a closed subscription accompanied by the registration of a securities prospectus an emitent shall be obliged to publish a communication concerning the State registration of the issue (or additional issue) of emission securities, in so doing having indicated the procedure for access of potential possessors of emission securities to information contained in the securities prospectus in a printed organ of the mass media distributed in a print-run of not less than 1000 examples [as amended by Federal Law No. 185-Ф3, 28 December 2002].

[paragraphs three to seven repealed by Federal Law No. 185-Ф3, 28 December 2002]

Article 24. Conditions of Placement of Emission Securities Issued

An emitent shall have the right to commence the placement of emission securities only after State registration of the issue thereof, unless established otherwise by the present Federal Law [as amended by Federal Law No. 185-Ф3, 28 December 2002].

The quantity of placed emission securities must not exceed the quantity specified in the decision concerning the issue (or additional issue) of emission securities [as amended by Federal Law No. 185-Ф3, 28 December 2002].

The emitent may place a lesser quantity of emission securities than was specified in the decision concerning the issue (or additional issue) of emission securities. The actual quantity of placed securities shall be specified in the report concerning the results of the issuance submitted for registration. The participatory share of the unplaced securities from among those specified in the decision concerning the issue (or additional issue) of emission securities under which the emission is considered to be unconstituted shall be established by the federal agency of executive power for the securities market [as amended by Federal Law No. 185-ФЗ, 28 December 2002].

The means of investors in the event of an unconstituted emission shall be returned in the procedure established by the federal agency of executive power for the securities market [as amended by Federal Law No. 185-ФЗ, 28 December 2002].

The emitent shall be obliged to complete the placement of emission securities issued not later than one year from the date of State registration of the issue (or additional issue) of such securities [as amended by Federal Law No. 185-ФЗ, 28 December 2002].

The placement by means of subscription to emission securities of an issue whose State registration is accompanied by the registration of a securities prospectus earlier than two weeks after publication of the communication concerning State registration of the issue of emission securities in accordance with Article 23 of the present Federal Law shall be prohibited. Information concerning the price of placement of emission securities may be disclosed on the day of the commencement of emission securities [as amended by Federal Law No. 185-ФЗ, 28 December 2002].

It shall be prohibited in the event of the public placement or circulation of the issue of emission securities to prefer one potential possessor over others when acquiring securities. The present provision shall not apply in the following instances:

(1) in the event of the emission of State securities;

(2) in the event of the granting to stockholders of joint-

stock societies a preferential right of purchase of a new emission of securities in a quantity proportional to the number of stocks belonging to them at the moment of the adoption of the decision concerning emission;

(3) in the event of the introduction by the emitent of limitations on the acquisition of securities by nonresidents.

Article 25. Report on Results of Issue (or Additional Issue) of Emission Securities [as amended by Federal Law No. 185-ФЗ, 28 December 2002]

Not later than 30 days after the completion of the placement of emission securities the emitent shall be obliged to submit a report concerning the results of the issue (or additional issue) of emission securities to the registering agency.

The report concerning the results of the issue (or additional issue) of emission securities must contain the following information:

(1) the date of commencement and ending of the placement of the securities;

(2) the actual price of placement of the securities (by types of securities within the framework of the particular issuance);

(3) the quantity of securities placed;

(4) the total amount of proceeds for the placed securities, including:

(a) the amount of monetary means in rubles as payment for placed securities;

(b) the amount of foreign currency as payment for placed securities expressed in currency of the Russian Federation at the exchange rate of the Central Bank of the Russian Federation at the moment of payment;

(c) the amount of material and nonmaterial assets as payment for placed securities expressed in the currency of the Russian Federation.

The list of possessors possessing a bloc of emission securities, the amount of which is determined by the federal agency of executive power for the securities market, shall be specified additionally for stocks in the report concerning the results of the issue (or additional issue) of emission securities.

Simultaneously with the report concerning the results of the issue (or additional issue) of emission securities an application shall be submitted to the registering agency concerning the registration thereof and documents confirming compliance by the emitent with the requirements of legislation of the Russian Federation determining the procedure and conditions for placement of the securities, confirmation of the report concerning the results of the issue of securities, disclosure of information, and other requirements, compliance with which is necessary when placing securities. An exhaustive list of such documents shall be determined by normative legal acts of the federal agency of executive power for the securities market [paragraph four added by Federal Law No. 185-ФЗ, 28 December 2002].

The registering agency shall consider the report concerning the results of the issue (or additional issue) of emission securities within a two-week period and in the absence of violations connected with the issue of securities, shall register it. The registering agency shall be liable for the completeness of the report registered by it.

Article 26. Emission Not in Good Faith

Actions expressed in a violation of the procedure for an emission established in the present Section which are grounds for a refusal by registering agencies of the State registration of an issue (or additional issue) of emission securities, deeming the issue of emission securities to be unconstituted, or suspension of the emission of emission securities shall be deemed to be an emission not in good faith [as amended by Federal Law

No. 185-ФЗ, 28 December 2002].

In the event of the discovery by a registering agency of the indicia of an emission not in good faith, it shall be obliged within seven days to communicate this to the federal agency of executive power for the securities market (regional division of federal agency of executive power for the securities market) [as amended by Federal Law No. 185-ФЗ, 28 December 2002].

The State registration of an issue (or additional issue) of emission securities may be refused when there are grounds provided for in Article 21 of the present Federal Law [as amended by Federal Law No. 185-ФЗ, 28 December 2002].

The issue of emission securities may be suspended or deemed to be unconstituted in the event of the discovery by the registering agency of the following violations:

violation by the emitent in the course of the emission of the requirements of legislation of the Russian Federation;

discovery in documents on the basis of which the issuance of securities was registered of unreliable information.

In the event of eliciting violations of the established procedure of an emission the registering agency may also suspend the emission until the elimination of violations within the limits of a period for placement of the securities. The renewal of the emission shall be effectuated according to a special decision of the registering agency.

In the event of the deeming of the issue of emission securities to be invalid, all securities of the particular issue shall be subject to return to the emitent, and the means received by the emitent from the placement of the issue of securities deemed to be invalid must be returned to the possessors. The federal agency of executive power for the securities market shall have the right to apply to a court for the return of the means to possessors [as amended by Federal Law No. 185-ФЗ, 28 December 2002].

All costs connected with deeming the issuance of emission securities to be invalid (or unconstituted) and return of means to possessors shall be relegated to the expense of the emitent.

In the event of a violation expressed in the issue of securities into circulation in excess of that declared in the securities prospectus, the emitent shall be obliged to ensure the purchase and cancellation of securities issued into circulation in excess of the quantity announced for issue [as amended by Federal Law No. 185-ФЗ, 28 December 2002].

If the emitent within two months does not ensure the purchase and cancellation of securities issued into circulation in excess of the quantity announced for issue, the federal agency of executive power for the securities market shall have the right to apply to a court concerning the recovery of the means unfoundedly received by the emitent [as amended by Federal Law No. 185-ФЗ, 28 December 2002].

The period of limitations for deeming invalid an issue (or additional issue) of emission securities, transactions concluded in the process of the placement of emission securities, and the report concerning the results of their issue shall comprise three months from the moment of registration of the report concerning the results of the issue (or additional issue) of these securities [paragraph added by Federal Law No. 185-ФЗ, 28 December 2002]

Article 27. Peculiarities of Emission of Stocks by Credit Organisations

The accumulation of means in the process of the emission of stocks by credit organisations shall be effectuated by the opening by the emitent bank of a cumulation account.

The regime of the cumulation account shall be established by the Central Bank of the Russian Federation.

Article 27¹. Peculiarities of Emission of Options of

Emitent [added by Federal Law No. 185-ФЗ, 28 December 2002]

An emitent shall not have the right to place options of the emitent if the quantity of declared stocks of the emitent is less than the quantity of stocks, the right to the acquisition of which grant such options.

The quantity of stocks of a determined category (or type), the right to the acquisition of which grants options of the emitent, may not exceed 5% of the stocks of this category (or type) placed on the date of submission of the documents for State registration of the issue of options of the emitent.

The decision concerning the issue of options of an emitent may provide for limitations on the circulation thereof.

The placement of options of the emitent shall be possible only after the paying up in full of the charter capital of a joint-stock society.

Article 27². Peculiarities of Emission and Circulation of Bonds With Security [added by Federal Law No. 185-ФЗ, 28 December 2002]

1. Bonds, the performance of obligations under which is secured by a pledge (hereinafter – bonds with pledge security), suretyship, bank guarantee, State or municipal guarantee) shall be deemed to be bonds with security.

To relations connected with securing the performance of obligations under bonds with the pledge of property of the emitent or a third person shall apply the provisions of the Civil Code of the Russian Federation and other federal laws, taking into account the peculiarities established by the present Federal Law.

A bond with security shall grant to the possessor thereof all rights arising from such security. With the transfer of rights to a bond with security shall pass all rights to the new possessor (or acquirer) arising from such security. The transfer of rights which arose from the security provided without the transfer of rights to the bond shall be invalid.

2. In the event of the emission of bonds with security the conditions of the secured obligation must be contained in the decision concerning the issue of bonds and, if in accordance with the present Federal Law, State registration of the issue of bonds is accompanied by the registration of a bond prospectus, in the bond prospectus, and in the event of the documentary form of the issue, also in the bond certificates.

3. If security with regard to bonds has been provided by a third person, the decision concerning the issue of bonds and/ or bond prospectus, and in the event of the documentary form of issue, also a certificate, must be signed also by the person who provided such security.

4. If security with regard to bonds has been provided by a foreign person, to the relations connected with the securing of bonds shall apply norms of law of the Russian Federation. All disputes which arose as a consequence of the failure to perform or improper performance by the person who provided the security of his duties shall be within the systemic jurisdiction of the courts of the Russian Federation.

Article 27³. Bonds with Pledge Security [added by Federal Law No. 185-ФЗ, 28 December 2002]

1. Only securities and immoveable property may be the subject of a pledge with regard to bonds with pledge security.

Property which is the subject of a pledge with regard to bonds with pledge security shall be subject to valuation by a valuer.

2. Each possessor of a bond with pledge security of one issue shall have rights equal with all other possessors of bonds of this same issue with respect to property which is the subject of pledge, and also insurance compensation and the amounts

of compensation due to the pledgor in the event of the withdrawal (or purchase) of pledged property for State or municipal needs and the requisition or nationalisation thereof.

3. A contract of pledge by which the performance is secured of obligations with regard to bonds shall be considered to be concluded from the moment of the arising with the first possessor (or acquirer) thereof of the rights to such bonds. In so doing the written form of the contract on pledge shall be considered to be complied with. If the performance of obligations under bonds is secured by the pledge of immoveable property (mortgage), demands concerning the notarial form of the contract of mortgage and the State registration thereof shall be considered to be complied with on condition of notarial certification and State registration by a justice institution of the decision concerning the issue of bonds with pledge security.

4. Notarial certification and State registration by a justice institution of a decision concerning the issue of bonds secured by a mortgage shall be effectuated after the State registration of the issue of such bonds. State registration of a mortgage shall be effectuated by a justice institution simultaneously with the State registration of the decision concerning the issue of bonds secured by the mortgage.

The placement of bonds secured by a mortgage before State registration of the mortgage shall be prohibited.

5. If the performance of obligations with regard to bonds is secured by a pledge of immoveable property (mortgage), for State registration of the mortgage, instead of a notarially certified contract concerning the mortgage and a copy thereof, and also a document confirming the arising of the obligation secured by the mortgage, there shall be submitted a notarially certified decision concerning the issue of bonds secured by a mortgage and a copy of such decision. In the event of the State registration of a mortgage as information concerning the initial pledgeholder the registration entry concerning the mortgage in the unified State register of rights to immoveable prop-

erty must contain the registration number of the issue of bonds and the date of State registration thereof, and also an indication that the possessors of bonds of the issue with the said State registration number are the pledgeholders.

In the event of the deeming of the issue of bonds secured by a pledge to be unconstituted, the registration entry concerning the mortgage shall be cancelled on the basis of an application of the pledgor, to which shall be appended a document confirming the adoption by the registering agency of a decision to deem the respective issue of bonds to be unconstituted.

6. If securities are not inscribed, they may be provided as security with regard to bonds only on condition of recording the rights thereto in a depositary.

7. If bonds have been secured by a pledge of securities, the rights to which have been recorded in the system of keeping a register (or in the register) or in a depositary, after the State registration of the issue of such bonds and before the commencement of their placement the pledgor shall be obliged to fix the encumberment of the securities by a pledge with the person effectuating the recording of rights to these securities and to submit evidence of such fixation in the agency effectuating State registration of the respective issue of bonds, with State registration of the report concerning the results of the issue.

8. In the event of the failure to perform or improper performance of obligations with regard to bonds with pledge security, property which is the subject of a pledge shall be subject to realisation upon the written demand of any of the possessors of such securities send to the pledgeholder, person specified in the decision concerning the issue as the person who will effectuate the realisation of the pledged property, and also to the emitent of such securities if the pledgor is a third person.

Possessors of bonds with pledge security shall have the right to declare the said demands within two months from the day of ensuing of the period of performance of the obligation (or expiry of the last day of the period if performance of obligations was provided for within a determined period of time).

Public sales with regard to the realisation of pledged property by which obligations have been secured with regard to bonds may not be conducted earlier than the expiry of the period established for the presentation of demands of possessors of the said bonds.

Monetary means received from the realisation of pledged property shall be sent to persons who are possessors of bonds with pledge security having the right to effectuate the rights certified by the said securities and who have declared their own demands during the period established by the present Article for sending demands concerning the realisation of pledged property or upon the expiry of that period, but not later than the last day of the period established by the decision concerning the issue of these securities for realisation of the pledged property. If the amount received in the event of realisation of pledged property exceeds the amount of demands secured by the pledge with regard to bonds, the difference after withholding the amounts therefrom necessary to cover expenses connected with the levy of execution against this property and the realisation thereof shall be returned to the pledgor. The amount received from realisation of pledged property and remaining after the satisfaction of the demands of possessors of bonds with pledge security within the said procedure not exceeding the amount of demands secured by the pledge with regard to bonds shall be subject to being credited to a deposit with a notary. Possessors who have not sent the said written demands concerning the realisation of pledged property and not received means from the realisation thereof shall have the right to receive them through the deposit with the notary in the procedure established by a law.

If on the grounds provided for by legislation of the Russian Federation pledged property must pass to the ownership of the possessors of bonds with pledge security, the property which is the subject of pledge with regard to bonds shall pass to the common participatory share ownership of all possessors of bonds secured by such pledge.

Article 27⁴. Bonds Secured by Suretyship [added by Federal Law No. 185-ФЗ, 28 December 2002]

A contract of suretyship by which the performance of obligations is secured with regard to bonds shall be considered to be concluded from the moment of the arising with the first possessor thereof of rights to such bonds. In so doing the written form of the contract of suretyship shall be considered to be complied with.

A contract of suretyship by which the performance of obligations is secured with regard to bonds may provide only for joint and several responsibility of the surety and the emitent for the failure to perform or improper performance by the emitent of obligations with regard to the bonds.

Article 27⁵. Bonds Secured by Bank Guarantee and State or Municipal Guarantee [added by Federal Law No. 185-ФЗ, 28 December 2002]

A bank guarantee provided to secure the performance of obligations with regard to bonds may not be revoked.

The period for which a bank guarantee is issued must not by more than six months exceed the date (or period of ending) of cancellation of the bonds secured by such guarantee.

It must be provided by the conditions of a bank guarantee that the rights of demand against the guarantor shall pass to the person to whom the rights to the bond pass.

A bank guarantee which is secured by the performance of obligations with regard to bonds must provide only for the

joint and several responsibility of the guarantor and emitent
for the failure to perform or improper performance by the
emitent of obligations with regard to the bonds.

State and municipal guarantees with regard to bonds
shall be provided in accordance with budget legislation of the
Russian Federation and legislation of the Russian Federation
on State (or municipal) securities.

Chapter 6. Circulation of Emission Securities

Article 27[6]. Limitations on Circulation of Emission Securities [added by Federal Law No. 185-ФЗ, 28 December 2002]

The circulation of emission securities before the paying
up thereof in full and State registration of the report concerning the results of their issue shall be prohibited. In so doing the
public circulation of emission securities, including securities of
foreign emitents, before registration of the securities prospectus shall be prohibited.

Article 28. Form of Certification of Right of Ownership to Emission Securities

The rights of possessors to emission securities of the documentary form of issuance shall be certified by certificates (if
certificates are situated with possessors) or by certificates and
entries in deposit accounts at depositaries (if the certificates
for transferred for keeping to the depositary).

The rights of possessors to emission securities of paperless
form of issue shall be certified in the system of keeping the
register by entries in personal accounts with the holder of the
register or in the event of the recording of rights to securities
at the depositary, by entries in the deposit accounts at the

depositaries.

Article 29. Transfer of Rights to Securities and Realisation of Rights Consolidated by Securities

The right to a bearer documentary security shall pass to the acquirer:

in the event of the certificate thereof being with the possessor: at the moment of transfer of this certificate to the acquirer;

in the event of the keeping of certificates of bearer documentary securities and/or recording of rights to such securities in a depositary: at the moment of effectuation of the arrival entry in the deposit account of the acquirer.

The right to an inscribed paperless security shall pass to the acquirer:

in the event of the recording of the rights to securities with the person effectuating depositary activity: from the moment of making the arrival entry in the deposit account of the acquirer;

in the event of the recording of the rights to securities in the system of keeping the register: from the moment of making the arrival entry in the personal account of the acquirer.

[paragraph three repealed by Federal Law No. 185-ФЗ, 28 December 2002]

The rights consolidated by an emission security shall pass to the acquirer thereof from the moment of transfer of the rights to this security. The transfer of the rights consolidated by an inscribed emission security must be accompanied by informing the holder of the register or the depositary or the nominee holder of the securities.

The rights relating to bearer emission securities shall be effectuated upon presentation by the possessor thereof or his entrusted person.

[paragraph six repealed by Federal Law No. 185-ФЗ,

28 December 2002]

In the event certificates of documentary emission securities are kept in depositaries, the rights consolidated by securities shall be effectuated on the basis of certificates presented by these depositaries under a commission of the possessors granted by depositary contracts with the list of such possessors appended. The emitent in this instance shall ensure the realisation of the rights relating to bearer securities of the person specified in this list.

The effectuation of rights relating to inscribed paperless emission securities shall be by the emitent with respect to the persons specified in the system of conducting the register.

If the data concerning the new possessor of such security was not communicated to the holder of the register of the particular issuance or to the nominee holder of the security at the moment of closing the register in order to execute the performance of obligations of the emitent comprising the security (voting, receipt of revenue, and others), the performance of obligations with respect to the possessor registered in the register at the moment of closure thereof shall be deemed to be proper. Responsibility for the timely notification lies on the acquirer of the security.

If by legislation of the Russian Federation or other normative legal acts of the Russian Federation limitations have been established on the participatory share of participation of foreign persons in the capital of Russian emitents, the conclusion of transactions with regard to the acquisition by foreign possessors of stocks issued by such Russian emitents, the parties under the transaction shall inform the federal agency of executive power for the securities market and other agencies in the instances provided for by federal laws [as amended by Federal Law No. 185-ФЗ, 28 December 2002].

[paragraph eleven repealed by Federal Law No. 185-ФЗ, 28 December 2002]

The authenticity of the signature of natural persons on

documents concerning the transfer of rights to securities and rights consolidated by securities (except for instances provided for by legislation of the Russian Federation) may be attested notarially or professional participant of the securities market.

Section IV. Informational Provision of Securities Market

Chapter 7. On Disclosure of Information on Securities

Article 30. Disclosure of Information

Disclosure of information shall be understood to be ensuring the accessibility thereof to all persons interested therein irrespective of the purpose of receiving the said information with regard to the procedure guaranteeing the location and receipt thereof.

Information with respect to which actions have been conducted with regard to disclosing it shall be deemed to be disclosed information on the securities market.

Generally-accessible information on the securities market shall be deemed to be information not requiring privileges for access thereto or subject to disclosure in accordance with the present Federal Law.

In the event of the registration of a securities prospectus the emitent shall be obliged to effectuate the disclosure of information in the form of:

the quarterly report of the emitent of emission securities (quarterly report);

a communication concerning material facts (or events, actions) affecting the financial-economic activity of the emitent of emission securities (communication concerning material facts) [as amended by Federal Law No. 185-ФЗ, 28 December 2002].

The quarterly report must contain information, the composition and amount of which corresponds to the requirements of the present Federal Law for a securities prospectus, except for information concerning the procedure and conditions of placement of emission securities [as amended by Federal Law No. 185-ФЗ, 28 December 2002].

The yearly bookkeeping report for the last completed financial year shall be included in the composition of the quarterly report for the first quarter [as amended by Federal Law No. 185-ФЗ, 28 December 2002].

In the event of drawing up a composite bookkeeping report of the emitent such bookkeeping report for the last completed financial year shall be included in the composition of the quarterly report for the second quarter [added by Federal Law No. 185-ФЗ, 28 December 2002].

The yearly bookkeeping report of the emitent, and also composite bookkeeping report of the emitent for two completed financial years preceding the last completed financial year, shall not be submitted in the composition of the quarterly report [added by Federal Law No. 185-ФЗ, 28 December 2002].

The bookkeeping report for the fourth quarter shall not be included in the quarterly report [added by Federal Law No. 185-ФЗ, 28 December 2002].

The quarterly report shall be submitted to the registering agency not later than 45 days from the date of the end of the reporting quarter [added by Federal Law No. 185-ФЗ, 28 December 2002].

The quarterly report must be signed by the person effectuating the functions of one-man executive organ of the emitent, the chief bookkeeper thereof (or other person fulfilling his functions), thereby confirming the reliability of all information contained therein. A quarterly report must be provided to possessions of emission securities of the emitent upon their request for payment not exceeding expenditures for the manufacture of brochures. Persons who have signed the quarterly report shall bear responsibility for the fullness and reliability of the information communicated therein [added by Federal Law No. 185-ФЗ, 28 December 2002].

Communications concerning material facts shall be deemed to be [as amended by Federal Law No. 185-ФЗ, 28 December 2002]:

information concerning the reorganisation of the emitent and its subsidiary and dependent societies;

information concerning facts which entailed the one-off increase or reduction of the value of assets of the emitent by more than 10%, concerning facts which entailed the one-off increase of net profit or net losses of the emitent of more than 10%, concerning facts of one-off transactions of the emitent, the amount of which or the value of the property with regard to which comprises 10% and more of the assets of the emitent as of the date of the transaction;

information concerning the issue by the emitent of securities and concerning credited and/or paid revenues with regard to securities of the emitent;

information concerning the emergence in the register of the emitent of a person possessing more than 25% of its emission securities of any individual type;

information concerning the dates of the closure of the register, the periods for the performance of obligations of the emitent to possessors, and decisions of general meetings;

information concerning the adoption by the empowered organ of the emitent of a decision concerning the issuance of emission securities.

Communications concerning material facts must be sent by the emitent to the federal agency of executive power for the securities market or agency empowered by it, and also shall be published by the emitent not later than five days from the moment of the ensuing of these facts in printed mass media disseminated by a print run accessible to the majority of possessors of securities of the emitent [as amended by Federal Law No. 185-ФЗ, 28 December 2002].

The possessor shall be obliged to effectuate the disclosure of information concerning its possession of emission securities of any emitent whatsoever, except for bonds not convertible into stocks, in the following instances [as amended by Federal Law No. 185-ФЗ, 28 December 2002]:

the possessor entered into possession of 20% or more of any type of emission securities of the emitent;

the possessor increased its participatory share of possession of any type of emission securities of the emitent up to a level by a multiple of 5% above the 20% of this type of securities;

the possessor reduced its participatory share of possession of any type of emission securities of the emitent up to a level by a multiple of 5% above 20% of this type of securities.

The possessor shall disclose the said information (containing the name of the possessor, type and State registration number of the securities, name of the emitent, quantity of securities belonging to it) not later than five days after the respective actions by means in notifying the federal agency of executive power for the securities market or agency empowered by it [as amended by Federal Law No. 185-ФЗ, 28 December 2002].

Professional participants of the securities market shall be obliged to effectuate the disclosure of information concerning its securities operations in the following instances:

the professional participant of the securities market performed operations within one quarter with a single type of securities of a single emitent, if the quantity of securities relating to these operations comprised not less than 100% of the total number of the said securities;

the professional participant of the securities market performed a one-off operation with a single type of securities of a single emitent, if the quantity of securities relating to this operation comprised not less than 15% of the total quantity of the said securities.

Professional participants of the securities market shall disclose the said information (containing the name of the professional participant of the securities market, type and State registration code of the securities, name of the emitent, price of one security, quantity of securities with regard to respective transactions) not later than five days after the end of the respective quarter or after the respective one-off operation by means of informing the federal agency of executive power for the securities market or agency empowered by it [as amended by Federal Law No. 185-ФЗ, 28 December 2002].

A professional participant of the securities market shall when offering and/or announcing prices for the purchase and/or sale of emission securities, be obliged to disclose generally accessible information which he has disclosed by the emitent of these emission securities or communicate the fact that he lacks such information.

The composition, procedure, and periods for the disclosure of information, and also the submission of reports by professional participants of the securities market, shall be determined by normative legal acts of the federal agency of executive power for the securities market [as amended by Federal Law No. 185-ФЗ, 28 December 2002].

Chapter 8. On Use of Employment Information on Securities Market

Article 31. Employment Information

Employment information for the purposes of the present Federal Law shall be deemed to be any information which is not generally accessible concerning the emitent and emission securities issued by it which places persons possessing such information by virtue of their employment position, labour duties, or a contract concluded with the emitent in a preferential position in comparison with other subjects of the securities market.

Article 32. On Persons Disposing of Employment Information

There shall be relegated to persons disposing of employment information:

members of the management organs of the emitent or professional participant of the securities market connected with this emitent by a contract;

[paragraph three repealed by Federal Law No. 185-ФЗ, 28 December 2002]

auditors of the emitent or professional participant of the securities market connected with this emitent by a contract;

employees of State agencies having by virtue of control, supervisory, and other powers access to the said information.

In so doing members of management organs of the emitent and a professional participant of the securities market shall be understood to be persons occupying posts permanently or temporarily which are connected with the fulfilment of organisational-administrative or administrative-economic duties, and also fulfilling such duties under a special power [as amended by Federal Law No. 185-ФЗ, 28 December 2002].

Article 33. Transactions Performed With Use of Employment Information

Persons disposing of employment information shall not have the right to use this information in order to conclude transactions, and also to transfer employment information to conclude transactions with third persons.

Persons who have violated the said requirement shall bear responsibility in accordance with legislation of the Russian Federation.

Chapter 9. On Advertising on the Securities Market

Article 34. Requirements for Advertising

An advertisement must contain the name of the advertiser. The advertiser who is a professional participant of the securities market shall also be obliged to include in the advertisement information concerning the types of activity effectuated by him on the securities market in accordance with the advertised announcement.

Advertisers shall be prohibited to:

specify in the advertisement reliable information concerning its activity and the types and characteristics of securities offered for purchase or sale or other transactions therewith and the conditions of such transactions and other information directed towards fraud or deceiving the possessors and other participants of the securities market;

specify in the advertisement the proposed amount of revenues with regard to the securities and the forecast of the growth of their rated value;

use the advertisement for the purposes of unfair competition by means of indicating real or fictitious shortcomings of professional participants of the securities market engaging in analogous activity or emitents issuing analogous securities.

When one of the circumstances specified in paragraph two of the present Article is present in an advertisement, the advertisement of the securities shall be deemed to be not in good faith.

The public guarantee or otherwise bringing to the information of potential possessors of data concerning the profitability of securities, ensuring thereof in comparison with other securities or other financial instruments, and also communicating information known to be false or unreliable capable of entailing or which entailed the deception of potential possessors relative to the securities being acquired shall be deemed to be an advertisement not in good faith.

The advertiser shall bear responsibility for damage caused by an advertisement not in good faith in accordance with legislation of the Russian Federation.

In the event of deeming an advertisement to be not in good faith, the contracts of the advertiser with the disseminator of the advertisement shall be invalid.

Article 35. On Information Which Is Not Advertising on Securities Market

Generally accessible information on securities and emitents specified in Article 30 of the present Federal Law, and also information granted to empowered agencies in connection with the fulfilment by them of functions relating to regulation of the securities market in accordance with legislation of the Russian Federation, shall not be advertising on the securities market.

Information concerning the issue by the emitent of securities and dividends calculated and/or paid shall be advertising.

Article 36. On Prohibition to Advertise Unregistered Issues of Emission Securities

The advertising of emission securities before the date of State registration of their issues (or additional issues) in accordance with legislation of the Russian Federation shall be prohibited. Contracts for advertising unregistered issues of emission securities shall be invalid. Agencies which effectuated the State registration of an issue (or additional issue) of emission securities shall have the right to bring a suit with regard to the consequences which have arisen because of the invalidity of the contracts [as amended by Federal Law No.

185-ФЗ, 28 December 2002].

Article 37. On Grounds for Termination of Contract for Advertising Emission Securities

The deeming of the issue of emission securities to be unconstituted shall be grounds for the termination of a contract for advertising these securities. The contract for advertising emission securities, the issue of which is deemed to be unconstituted, shall terminate from the moment of notification of the advertisement disseminator by the registering agency which has deemed the issue of emission securities to be unconstituted. The advertisement disseminator shall have the right to demand from the advertiser compensation of losses caused as a result of the termination of the contract for advertising.

Section V. Regulation of Securities Market

Chapter 10. Foundations of Regulation of Securities Market

Article 38. Foundations of Regulation of Securities Market

State regulation of the securities market shall be effectuated by means of:

the establishment of obligatory requirements for the activity of emitents, professional participants of the securities market, and standards thereof;

the State registration of issues of emission securities and securities prospectuses and control over compliance by emitents with the conditions and obligations provided for therein [as amended by Federal Law No. 185-ФЗ, 28 December 2002];

the licensing of the activity of professional participants

of the securities market;

the creation of a system for the defence of the rights of possessors and control over compliance with their rights by emitents and professional participants of the securities market;

the prohibitions and suppression of the activity of persons effectuating entrepreneurial activity on the securities market without a respective license.

Representative agencies of State power and agencies of local self-government shall establish maximum amounts of the emission of securities emitted by agencies of power of the respective level.

Chapter 11. Regulation of Activity of Professional Participants of Securities Market

Article 39. Licensing of Activity of Professional Participants of Securities Market

All types of professional activity on the securities market specified in Chapter 2 of the present Federal Law shall be effectuated on the basis of a special authorisation – a license issued by the federal agency of executive power for the securities market or agencies empowered by it on the basis of a general license [as amended by Federal Law No. 185-ФЗ, 28 December 2002].

Credit organisations shall effectuate professional activity on the securities market in the procedure established by the present Federal Law for professional participants of the securities market. An additional ground for refusal to issue a license to a credit organisation for the effectuation of professional activity on the securities market, suspension or annulment thereof shall be the annulment or revocation of a license for the effectuation of banking operations issued by the Bank of Russia [as amended by Federal Law No. 185-ФЗ, 28 December 2002].

The agencies which issued the license shall control the activity of professional participants of the securities market and shall adopt a decision concerning the revocation of the license issued in the event of a violation of legislation of the Russian Federation on securities.

The activity of professional participants of the securities market shall be licensed by three types of licenses: the license of a professional participant of the securities market; the license to effectuate activity with regard to keeping the register; and the license of the stock exchange.

A condition of the rendering of services by the broker and/or dealer with regard to the preparation of a securities prospectus shall be the conformity thereof to the requirements established by normative legal acts of the federal agency of executive power for the securities market to the extent of own capital and skills requirements for personnel (or workers) [added by Federal Law No. 185-ФЗ, 28 December 2002].

Chapter 12. Federal Agency of Executive Power for Securities Market
[as amended by Federal Law No. 185-ФЗ, 28 December 2002]

Article 40. Organisation of Federal Agency of Executive Power for Securities Market [as amended by Federal Law No. 185-ФЗ, 28 December 2002]

The federal agency of executive power for the securities market shall be the federal agency of executive power for conducting State policy in the domain of the securities market, control over the activity of professional participants of the securities market through the determination of the procedure for their activity and determination of the standards of the emission of securities [as amended by Federal Law No. 185-ФЗ, 28 December 2002].

The director of the federal agency of executive power for the securities market shall be ex officio a federal minister [as amended by Federal Law No. 185-ФЗ, 28 December 2002].

The posts of five members of the federal agency of executive power for the securities market (first deputy chairman, deputy chairmen of the federal agency of executive power for the securities market, secretary of the federal agency of executive power for the securities market) shall be State posts of the State service and shall be filled in the established procedure [as amended by Federal Law No. 185-ФЗ, 28 December 2002].

The basic functions and powers of the federal agency of executive power for the securities market shall be determined by the present Federal Law [as amended by Federal Law No. 185-ФЗ, 28 December 2002].

The federal agency of executive power for the securities market shall in order to effectuate its powers create its own territorial agencies [as amended by Federal Law No. 185-ФЗ, 28 December 2002].

The powers of the federal agency of executive power for the securities market shall not extend to the procedure for the emission of debt obligations of the Government of the Russian Federation and securities of subjects of the Russian Federation [as amended by Federal Law No. 185-ФЗ, 28 December 2002].

Article 41. Collegium of Federal Agency of Executive Power for Securities Market [as amended by Federal Law No. 185-ФЗ, 28 December 2002]

The collegium of the federal agency of executive power for the securities market shall consist of 15 members, including the chairman of the federal agency of executive power for the securities market, the first deputy and deputy chairmen of the federal agency of executive power for the securities market, and the secretary of the federal agency of executive power for the securities market [as amended by Federal Law No. 185-ФЗ, 28 December 2002].

Five members of the collegium of the federal agency of executive power for the securities market shall be representatives of federal agencies of executive power within whose competence are questions connected with the securities market. The representative of the Ministry of Finances of the Russian Federation shall be obligatorily included in the membership thereof [as amended by Federal Law No. 185-ФЗ, 28 December 2002].

One member of the collegium of the federal agency of executive power for the securities market shall be a representative of the Central Bank of the Russian Federation [as amended by Federal Law No. 185-ФЗ, 28 December 2002].

The chairman of the Expert Council attached to the federal agency of executive power for the securities market shall be a member of the collegium of the federal agency of executive power for the securities market ex officio [as amended by Federal Law No. 185-ФЗ, 28 December 2002].

Two members of the collegium of the federal agency of executive power for the securities market shall be representatives of the chambers of the Federal Assembly of the Russian Federation [as amended by Federal Law No. 185-ФЗ, 28 December 2002].

A consultative-advisory organ – Expert Council attached to the federal agency of executive power for the securities market – shall be created by the federal agency of executive power for the securities market and shall have 25 members: representatives of State agencies and organisations whose activity is connected with the regulation of the financial market and the securities market, professional participants of the securities market, self-regulating organisations of professional participants of the securities market, unions and associations thereof, and other social associations and independent experts [as amended by Federal Law No. 185-ФЗ, 28 December 2002].

A member of the Expert Council attached to the federal agency of executive power for the securities market shall be appointed for a term of two years with the possibility of appointment any number of times [as amended by Federal Law No. 185-ФЗ, 28 December 2002].

Work in the collegium of the federal agency of executive power for the securities market and the Expert Council attached to the federal agency of executive power for the securities market of representatives of State agencies and other organisations specified in the present Article shall be effectuated on an uncompensated basis [as amended by Federal Law No. 185-ФЗ, 28 December 2002].

The collegium of the federal agency of executive power for the securities market autonomously shall confirm the Reglament of work and activity of the Expert Council attached to the federal agency of executive power for the securities market.

Article 42. Functions of Federal Agency of Executive Power for Securities Market [as amended by Federal Law No. 185-ФЗ, 28 December 2002]

The federal agency of executive power for the securities market shall [as amended by Federal Law No. 185-ФЗ, 28 December 2002]:

(1) effectuate the working out of the basic orientations of the development of the securities market and coordination of the activity of federal agencies of executive power for the securities market with regard to questions of the regulation of the securities market [as amended by Federal Law No. 185-ФЗ, 28 December 2002];

(2) confirm the standards for the emission of securities,

securities prospectuses of emitents, including foreign emitents effectuating the emission of securities on the territory of the Russian Federation and the procedure for the State registration of the issue (or additional issue) of emission securities, State registration of reports concerning the results of the issue (or additional issue) of emission securities, and the registration of securities prospectuses [as amended by Federal Law No. 185-ФЗ, 28 December 2002];

(3) work out and confirm unified requirements for rules for the effectuation of professional securities activity;

(4) establish obligatory requirements for securities operations, norms for the access of securities for public placement, circulation, quotation and listing, and settlement and depositary activity. The rules for keeping records and drawing up reports by emitents and professional participants of the securities market shall be established by the federal agency of executive power for the securities market jointly with the Ministry of Finances of the Russian Federation [as amended by Federal Law No. 185-ФЗ, 28 December 2002];

(5) establish obligatory requirements for the procedure of conducting the register;

(6) establish the procedure and effectuate the licensing of various types of professional activity on the securities market, and also suspend and annul the said licenses in the event of a violation of the requirements of legislation of the Russian Federation on securities;

(7) issue general licenses for the effectuation of activity with regard to the licensing of activity of professional participants of the securities market, and also suspend or annul the said licenses. The annulment of a general license issued to the empowered agency shall not entail the annulment of licenses issued by it to the professional participants of the securities market;

(8) establish the procedure, effectuate licensing, and conduct the register of self-regulating organisations of professional

participants of the securities market and annul the said licenses in the event of a violation of the requirements of legislation of the Russian Federation on securities, and also standards and requirements confirmed by the federal agency of executive power for the securities market [as amended by Federal Law No. 185-ФЗ, 28 December 2002];

(9) determine the standards of activity of investment, non-State pension and insurance funds and their management companies, and also of insurance companies, on the securities market;

(10) effectuate control over compliance by emitents, professional participants of the securities market, and self-regulating organisations of professional participants of the securities market with the requirements of legislation of the Russian Federation on securities, standards, and requirements confirmed by the federal agency of executive power for the securities market [as amended by Federal Law No. 185-ФЗ, 28 December 2002];

(11) for the purposes of counteracting the legalisation (or laundering) of revenues received by criminal means, control the procedure for conducting operations with monetary means or other property performed by professional participants of the securities market [added by Federal Law No. 121-ФЗ, 7 August 2002];

(12) ensure the disclosure of information concerning registered issues of securities, professional participants of the securities market, and the regulation of the securities market;

(13) ensure the creation of a generally-accessible system for the disclosure of information on the securities market;

(14) confirm the qualifications requirements for executives and personnel (or workers) of professional participants of the securities market, effectuate the attestation thereof (or verification of conformity to qualifications of executives and workers to the qualification requirements) in the form of taking a qualifications examination and issuing a qualifications

attestation, determine the procedure for conducting attestation, list of documents to be filed together with the application concerning admittance to attestation, quantity and types of attestants, syllabus of qualifications examination, and the procedure for taking it [as amended by Federal Law No. 185-ФЗ, 28 December 2002];

(15) work out draft legislative and other normative acts connected with questions of regulation of the securities market, licensing the activity of the professional participants thereof, and self-regulating organisations of professional participants of the securities market, control over compliance with legislative and normative acts on securities, and conduct the expert examination thereof;

(16) work out recommendations with regard to the application of legislation of the Russian Federation regulating relations connected with the functioning of the securities market [as amended by Federal Law No. 185-ФЗ, 28 December 2002];

(17) effectuate the direction of regional divisions of the federal agency of executive power for the securities market [as amended by Federal Law No. 185-ФЗ, 28 December 2002];

(18) conduct the register of issued, suspended, and annulled licenses;

(19) establish and determine the procedure for admittance to primary placement and circulation outside the territory of the Russian Federation of securities issued by emitents registered in the Russian Federation;

(20) apply to the arbitrazh court with a suit concerning the liquidation of a juridical person which has violated the requirements of legislation of the Russian Federation concerning securities and concerning the application to offenders of the sanctions established by legislation of the Russian Federation;

(21) effectuate supervision over the conformity of the amount of the issue of emission securities to the quantity thereof

in circulation;

(22) [repealed by Federal Law No. 185-ФЗ, 28 December 2002].

Article 43. Decisions of Federal Agency of Executive Power for Securities Market [as amended by Federal Law No. 185-ФЗ, 28 December 2002]

The federal agency of executive power for the securities market shall adopt decisions with regard to questions of the regulation of the securities market, the activity of professional participants of the securities market, self-regulating organisations of professional participants of the securities market, and control over compliance with legislation of the Russian Federation and normative acts on securities [as amended by Federal Law No. 185-ФЗ, 28 December 2002].

Decisions of the federal agency of executive power for the securities market shall be adopted in the form of decrees [as amended by Federal Law No. 185-ФЗ, 28 December 2002].

Decrees adopted by the federal agency of executive power for the securities market shall be signed by the chairman of the federal agency of executive power for the securities market, and in his absence, by his first deputy [as amended by Federal Law No. 185-ФЗ, 28 December 2002].

Protocols of the federal agency of executive power for the securities market shall be signed by the chairman of the federal agency of executive power for the securities market and by the secretary of the federal agency of executive power for the securities market [as amended by Federal Law No. 185-ФЗ, 28 December 2002].

Members of the federal agency of executive power for the securities market shall have the right to submit their opinion with regard to individual questions in the protocol, and also append to the protocol in written form a special opinion and individual materials [as amended by Federal Law No. 185-

ФЗ, 28 December 2002].

The preparation and adoption of documents in which a credit organisation is specially singled out by the federal agency of executive power for the securities market shall be by agreement with the Central Bank of the Russian Federation [as amended by Federal Law No. 185-ФЗ, 28 December 2002].

The operations with currency exchange valuables shall be regulated by the federal agency by agreement with the Central Bank of the Russian Federation [as amended by Federal Law No. 185-ФЗ, 28 December 2002].

Decrees of the federal agency of executive power for the securities market with regard to questions relegated to its competence binding for execution by federal ministries and other federal agencies of executive power, agencies of executive power of subjects of the Russian Federation, and agencies of local self-government, and also professional participants of the securities market and self-regulating organisations [as amended by Federal Law No. 185-ФЗ, 28 December 2002].

The adoption of decrees of the federal agency of executive power for the securities market without preliminary consideration thereof at the Expert Council attached to the federal agency of executive power for the securities market shall not be permitted [as amended by Federal Law No. 185-ФЗ, 28 December 2002].

Decrees of the federal agency of executive power for the securities market shall be subject to obligatory publication [as amended by Federal Law No. 185-ФЗ, 28 December 2002].

Decrees of the federal agency of executive power for the securities market having a normative character shall be subject to State registration in the instances and in the procedure which has been provided for normative legal acts of federal agencies of executive power [added by Federal Law No. 182-ФЗ, 26 November 1998, as amended by Federal Law No. 185-ФЗ, 28 December 2002].

Decrees of the federal agency of executive power for the securities market having a normative character shall enter into force upon the expiry of ten days from the day of their official publication unless another period for their entry into force has been provided for in those decrees [added by Federal Law No. 182-ФЗ, 26 November 1998, as amended by Federal Law No. 185-ФЗ, 28 December 2002].

Decrees of the federal agency of executive power for the securities market may be appealed by natural and juridical persons to a court or arbitrazh court [as amended by Federal Law No. 185-ФЗ, 28 December 2002].

Normative acts with regard to questions of the regulation of the securities market, the activity of professional participants of the securities market, and self-regulating organisations of professional participants of the securities market shall be adopted by federal ministries and other federal agencies of executive power within the limits of their competence only by agreement with the federal agency of executive power for the securities market [as amended by Federal Law No. 185-ФЗ, 28 December 2002].

Article 44. Rights of Federal Agency of Executive Power for Securities Market [as amended by Federal Law No. 185-ФЗ, 28 December 2002]

The federal agency of executive power for the securities market shall have the right to [as amended by Federal Law No. 185-ФЗ, 28 December 2002]:

(1) issue general licenses for the effectuation of licensing of professional participants of the securities market, and also for the effectuation of control over the securities market, to federal agencies of executive power (with the right to delegate functions relating to licensing to their territorial agencies);

(2) classify securities and determine their types in accordance with legislation of the Russian Federation;

(3) establish normative standards which are binding upon professional participants of the securities market, except for credit organisations, for sufficiency of own means and other requirements directed towards reducing risks of professional activity on the securities market, and also excluding conflicts of interests, including in the event of the rendering by a broker who is a financial consultant of services with regard to the placement of emission securities [as amended by Federal Law No. 185-ФЗ, 28 December 2002];

(4) in the event of a repeated violation within one year by professional participants of the securities market of legislation of the Russian Federation concerning securities, adopt a decision concerning the suspension of the operation or annulment of the license for the effectuation of professional activity on the securities market. Immediately after the entry into force of a decision of the federal agency of executive power for the securities market concerning the suspension of the operation of the license, the State agency which issued the respective license must adopt measures with regard to the elimination of violations or annul the license [as amended by Federal Law No. 185-ФЗ, 28 December 2002];

in the event of a repeated violation within one year by professional participants of the securities market of demands provided for by Articles 6 and 7 (except for Article 7(3)) of the Federal Law "On Counteracting the Legalisation (of Laundering) of Revenues Received by Criminal Means", adopt a decision concerning annulment of the license for the effectuation of professional activity on the securities market [as amended by Federal Law No. 121-ФЗ, 7 August 2001];

(5) on the grounds provided for by legislation of the Russian Federation, refuse to issue a license to a self-regulating organisation of professional participants of the securities market and annul the license issued to it with obligatory publication of a communication thereof in the mass media;

(6) establish the procedure for conducting verifications

of emitents, professional participants of the securities market, and self-regulating organisations of professional participants of the securities market, and also other organisations licensed by it, effectuate autonomously or jointly with respective federal agencies of executive power the verification of the activity of emitents, professional participants of the securities market, and self-regulating organisations of professional participants of the securities market, and also other organisations licensed by it, and appoint and recall inspectors for control over the activity of the said organisations [as amended by Federal Law No. 185-ФЗ, 28 December 2002];

(7) send to emitents and professional participants of the securities market, and also to their self-regulating organisations, prescriptions binding for execution and also demand from them the submission of documents necessary in order to decide questions within the competence of the federal agency of executive power for the securities market [as amended by Federal Law No. 185-ФЗ, 28 December 2002];

(8) send materials to law enforcement agencies and apply with suits to a court (or arbitrazh court) with regard to questions relegated to the competence of the federal agency of executive power for the securities market (including the invalidity of securities transactions) [as amended by Federal Law No. 185-ФЗ, 28 December 2002];

(9) adopt decisions concerning the creation and liquidation of regional divisions of the federal agency of executive power for the securities market [as amended by Federal Law No. 185-ФЗ, 28 December 2002];

(10) annul qualifications attestations of natural persons in the event of the repeated or flagrant violation by them of legislation of the Russian Federation on securities [as amended by Federal Law No. 185-ФЗ, 28 December 2002];

(11) establish normative standards obligatory for compliance by emitents of securities and the rules for the application thereof.

Article 44¹. Duties of Federal Agency of Executive Power for Securities Market [added by Federal Law No. 185-ФЗ, 28 December 2002]

When effectuating the powers granted by the present Federal Law, the federal agency of executive power for the securities market shall be obliged to:

(1) ensure the confidentiality of information provided to it, except for information disclosed in accordance with legislation of the Russian Federation on securities;

(2) when sending to emitents, professional participants of the securities market, and self-regulating organisations of professional participants of the securities market queries concerning the provision of information to substantiate with reasons the necessity to receive the information requested;

(3) effectuate the registration of documents of professional participants of the securities market and self-regulating organisations of professional participants of the securities market subject to registration in accordance with the present Federal Law not later than 30 days from the date of receipt of the respective documents or to provide within the said period a reasoned refusal of registration unless other periods for registration have been established by the present Federal Law;

(4) provide within 30 days reasoned replies to queries of juridical persons and citizens with regard to questions relegated to the competence of the federal agency of executive power for the securities market.

Article 45. Expert Council Attached to Federal Agency of Executive Power for Securities Market [as amended by Federal Law No. 185-ФЗ, 28 December 2002]

Professional participants of the securities market shall elect their candidates to the Expert Council attached to the federal agency of executive power for the securities market at the All-Russian Conference of Professional Participants of the Securities Market, organised by the federal agency of executive power for the securities market [as amended by Federal Law No. 185-ФЗ, 28 December 2002].

Candidates elected by professional participants of the securities market shall be confirmed as members of the Expert Council attached to the federal agency of executive power for the securities market by decision of the federal agency of executive power for the securities market [as amended by Federal Law No. 185-ФЗ, 28 December 2002].

The chairman of the Expert Council attached to the federal agency of executive power for the securities market shall be elected by the members of the Expert Council and shall be confirmed by the chairman of the federal agency of executive power for the securities market [as amended by Federal Law No. 185-ФЗ, 28 December 2002].

The procedure for the submission of candidacies for election as member of the Expert Council attached to the federal agency of executive power for the securities market from professional participants of the securities market and the conducting and totalling of the results of voting shall be established by decision of the All-Russian Conference of Professional Participants of the Securities Market [as amended by Federal Law No. 185-ФЗ, 28 December 2002].

Candidates for the Expert Council attached to the federal agency of executive power for the securities market from State agencies shall be submitted by these State agencies and shall be confirmed by decision of the federal agency of executive power for the securities market [as amended by Federal Law No. 185-ФЗ, 28 December 2002].

The Expert Council attached to the federal agency of executive power for the securities market shall effectuate [as amended by Federal Law No. 185-ФЗ, 28 December 2002]:

the preparation and preliminary consideration of questions connected with the execution of powers of the federal agency of executive power for the securities market [as amended by Federal Law No. 185-ФЗ, 28 December 2002];

the working out of proposals with regard to the basic orientations of regulation of the securities market;

the preliminary consideration of draft decrees to be adopted by the federal agency of executive power for the securities market, and their publication at the demand of any member of the Expert Council attached to the federal agency of executive power for the securities market [as amended by Federal Law No. 185-ФЗ, 28 December 2002].

The Expert Council attached to the federal agency of executive power for the securities market shall have the right by a majority vote of its members to suspend for a term of up to six months the introduction into operation of decrees of the federal agency of executive power for the securities market [as amended by Federal Law No. 185-ФЗ, 28 December 2002].

Article 46. Ensuring Activity of Federal Agency of Executive Power for Securities Market [as amended by Federal Law No. 185-ФЗ, 28 December 2002]

The activity of the federal agency of executive power for the securities market shall be ensured by the working apparatus [as amended by Federal Law No. 185-ФЗ, 28 December 2002].

The expenses connected with the activity of the federal agency of executive power for the securities market shall be effectuated at the expense of means of the federal budget directed towards the maintenance of federal agencies of executive power [as amended by Federal Law No. 185-ФЗ, 28 December 2002].

The federal agency of executive power for the securities market shall be a juridical person and have a seal depicting the State Arms of the Russian Federation and its own name [as amended by Federal Law No. 185-Ф3, 28 December 2002].

The federal agency of executive power for the securities market shall have a settlement account and other accounts, including hard currency [as amended by Federal Law No. 185-Ф3, 28 December 2002].

The location of the federal agency of executive power for the securities market shall be the City of Moscow [as amended by Federal Law No. 185-Ф3, 28 December 2002].

Article 47. Regional Divisions of Federal Agency of Executive Power for Securities Market [as amended by Federal Law No. 185-Ф3, 28 December 2002]

Regional divisions of the federal agency of executive power for the securities market shall be formed by decision of the federal agency of executive power for the securities market by agreement with agencies of executive power of subjects of the Russian Federation in order to ensure the fulfilment of the norms, rules, and conditions established by legislation of the Russian Federation for the functioning of the stock market, the practical realisation of decisions to be adopted by the federal agency of executive power for the securities market, and control over activity of professional participants of the securities market [as amended by Federal Law No. 185-Ф3, 28 December 2002].

A regional division of the federal agency of executive power for the securities market shall operate on the basis of a Statute confirmed by the federal agency of executive power for the securities market [as amended by Federal Law No. 185-Ф3, 28 December 2002].

The chairman of a regional division shall be confirmed by the federal agency of executive power for the securities market on the basis of the joint recommendation of the head of executive power of the subject of the Russian Federation and the chairman of the federal agency of executive power for the securities market [as amended by Federal Law No. 185-ФЗ, 28 December 2002].

Chapter 13. Self-Regulating Organisations of Professional Participants of the Securities Market

Article 48. Concept of Self-Regulating Organisation of Professional Participants of Securities Market

A voluntary association of professional participants of the securities market acting in accordance with the present Federal Law and functioning on the principles of a non-commercial organisation shall be called a self-regulating organisation of professional participants of the securities market (hereinafter: self-regulating organisation).

A self-regulating organisation shall be founded by professional participants of the securities market in order to ensure the conditions of professional activity of participants of the securities market, compliance with the standards of professional ethics on the securities market, defence of the interests of the possessors of securities and other clients of professional participants of the securities market who are members of the self-regulating organization, the establishment of rules and standards for conducting securities operations, and ensuring the effective activity of the securities market.

All revenues of the self-regulating organisation shall be used by it exclusively in order to fulfil the charter tasks and shall not be distributed among its members.

A self-regulating organisation shall, in accordance with the requirements for the effectuation of professional activity and the conducting of securities operations which are confirmed by the federal agency of executive power for the securities market, establish rules binding upon its members for the effectuation of professional activity on the securities market and standards for conducting securities operations and effectuate control over compliance therewith [as amended by Federal Law No. 185-ФЗ, 28 December 2002].

Article 49. Rights of Self-Regulating Organisations in Regulating Securities Market

A self-regulating organisation shall have the right to:

receive information relating to the results of verifications of the activity of their members effectuated in the procedure established by the federal agency of executive power for the securities market (or regional division of the federal agency of executive power for the securities market) [as amended by Federal Law No. 185-ФЗ, 28 December 2002];

work out in accordance with the present Federal Law the rules and standards for the effectuation of professional activity and securities operations by their members and effectuate control over compliance therewith;

control compliance by their members with the rules and standards adopted by the self-regulating organization for the effectuation of professional activity and securities operations;

in accordance with the qualifications requirements of the federal agency of executive power for the securities market, work out instructional syllabi and plans, effectuate the training of officials and personnel of organisations effectuating professional activity on the securities market, determine the qualifications of the said persons, and issue them qualifications attestations [as amended by Federal Law No. 185-ФЗ, 28 December 2002].

Article 50. Requirements for Self-Regulating Organisations

An organisation founded by not less than ten professional participants of the securities market shall have the right to file a statement at the federal agency of executive power for the securities market concerning the acquisition thereof of the status of a self-regulating organisation [as amended by Federal Law No. 185-ФЗ, 28 December 2002].

An organisation created by professional participants of the securities market shall acquire the status of a self-regulating organization on the basis of an authorisation issued by the federal agency of executive power for the securities market. The authorisation issued by the federal agency of executive power for the securities market to a self-regulating organisation shall include all the rights provided for by the present Article [as amended by Federal Law No. 185-ФЗ, 28 December 2002].

In order to receive an authorisation there shall be submitted to the federal agency of executive power for the securities market [as amended by Federal Law No. 185-ФЗ, 28 December 2002]:

certified copies of documents concerning the creation of the self-regulating organisation;

the rules and statutes of the organisation adopted by its members and obligatory for execution by all members of the self-regulating organisation.

The rules and statutes of a self-regulating organisation must contain the requirements for a self-regulating organisation and its members with respect to:

(1) the professional qualification of personnel (except technical);

(2) the rules and standards for the effectuation of professional activity;

(3) the rules limiting the manipulation of prices;

(4) documentation, the keeping of records and reports;

(5) the minimum amount of their own means;

(6) the rules for a professional participant of the securities market joining the organisation and with withdrawal or expulsion therefrom;

(7) equal rights to representation in elections to management organs of the organisation and participation in the management of the organisation;

(8) the procedure for the distribution of costs, payments, and fees among members of the organisation;

(9) defence of the rights of clients, including the procedure for the consideration of claims and appeals of clients of members of the organisation;

(10) obligations of its members with respect to clients and other persons in regard to compensation of damage by reason of mistakes or omissions when a member of the organisation is effectuating its professional activity, and also unlawful actions of a member of the organisation or its officials and/or personnel;

(11) compliance with the procedure for the consideration of claims and appeals of members of the organisation;

(12) procedure for conducting verifications of compliance by members of the organisation with the established rules and standards, including the creation of a control organ and the procedure for familiarisation with the results of the verifications of other members of the organisation;

(13) sanctions and other measures with respect to members of the organisation and their officials and/or other personnel and the procedure for applying them;

(14) requirements relating to ensuring openness of information for verifications to be conducted at the initiative of the organisation;

(15) control over the execution of sanctions and measures to be applied to members of the organisation and the procedure for recording them.

A self-regulating organisation which is an organiser of trade shall be obliged, in addition to the requirements provided for by point 3 of the present Article and by Article 10 of the present Federal Law, to establish and comply with rules for:

the conclusion, registration, and confirmation of securities transactions;

the conducting of operations ensuring securities trades (clearing and/or account settlement operations);

the formalisation and recording of documents to be used by members of the organisation when concluding transactions and conducting securities operations;

the settlement of disputes arising between members of the organisation when performing securities operations and the settlement of accounts with regard to them, including monetary;

procedures for the provision of information concerning the prices of demands and offers, concerning prices, and concerning the volume of securities transactions performed by members of the organisation;

rendering services to persons who are not members of the organisation.

The issuance of an authorisation may be refused if the documents submitted by the organisation of professional participants of the securities market do not contain even one the respective requirements enumerated in the present Article, as well as any of the following provisions which provide for:

the possibility of discrimination against the rights of clients who use the services of members of the organisation;

unsubstantiated discrimination against members of the organisation;

unsubstantiated limitation on joining the organisation or withdrawing from it;

limitations obstructing the development of competition of professional participants of the securities market, including the regulation of rates of remuneration and revenues from the professional activity of members of the organisation;

the regulation of questions not relegated to the competence nor corresponding to the purposes of the activity of a self-regulating organisation;

the granting of unreliable or incomplete information.

A refusal to issue an authorisation on other grounds shall not be permitted.

The authorisation of a self-regulating organisation shall be revoked in the event of the establishment by the federal agency of executive power for the securities market of violations of legislation of the Russian Federation on securities, the requirements and standards established by the federal agency of executive power for the securities market, the rules and statutes of the self-regulating organisation, and the granting of unreliable or incomplete information [as amended by Federal Law No. 185-ФЗ, 28 December 2002].

The self-regulating organisation shall be obliged to submit to the federal agency of executive power for the securities market data concerning all changes to be made in the documents concerning the creation and the statutes and rules of the self-regulating organisation with a brief substantiation of the reasons and purposes for such changes [as amended by Federal Law No. 185-ФЗ, 28 December 2002].

Changes and additions shall be considered to be adopted if within 30 calendar days from the moment of their receipt by the federal agency of executive power for the securities market a written notification has not been sent concerning a refusal, specifying the reasons therefor [as amended by Federal Law No. 185-ФЗ, 28 December 2002].

Section VI. Concluding Provisions

Article 51. Responsibility for Violation of Legislation of Russian Federation on Securities

1. Persons shall bear responsibility for a violation of the present Federal Law and other legislative acts of the Russian Federation on securities in the instances and procedure provided for by civil, administrative, or criminal legislation of the

Russian Federation.

The harm caused as a result of a violation of legislation of the Russian Federation on securities shall be subject to compensation in the procedure established by civil legislation of the Russian Federation.

2. Professional participants of the securities market shall not have the right to manipulate prices on the securities market nor to compel the purchase or sale of securities by means of granting deliberately distorted information on securities, the emitents of emission securities, and prices for securities, including information presented in an advertisement.

By manipulation of prices is understood actions committed for the creation of the appearance of raising and/or reducing prices and/or trading activeness on the securities market relative to the existing level of prices and/or existing trading activeness on the securities market for the purpose of persuading investors to sell or to acquire publicly placed and/or publicly circulated securities, including:

the dissemination of false or unreliable information;

the conclusion of securities transactions in public sales of stock exchanges and other organisers of trade on the securities market, as a result of which the possessor of these securities does not change;

the simultaneous placing of commissions for purchase and sale of securities at prices having a material deviation from current market prices under analogous transactions;

an agreement of two or several participants of a public sale or representatives thereof concerning the purchase (or sale) of securities at prices having material deviation from current market prices under analogous transactions [paragraphs two to six added by Federal Law No. 185-ФЗ, 28 December 2002].

The commission of the said actions by professional participants of the securities market shall be grounds for the suspension or annulment of the authorisation issued thereto, and also other sanctions provided for members of self-regulating organisations.

In the event of the discovery of facts giving grounds to suppose the presence in the actions of persons of the indicia of the manipulation of prices determined by the present point the federal agency of executive power for the securities market shall conduct a verification of the said facts in the procedure established by legislation of the Russian Federation and normative legal acts of the federal agency of executive power for the securities market. With regard to the results of the verification conducted and taking into account the explanations of the said persons the federal agency of executive power for the securities market shall render a decision concerning the deeming of a fact of manipulation of prices on the securities market and bring the guilty person(s) to responsibility provided for by legislation of the Russian Federation and/or suspension (or annulment) of the license issued to a professional participant of the securities market who is guilty of manipulation of prices or sending the materials of the verification to law enforcement agencies [as amended by Federal Law No. 185-ФЗ, 28 December 2002].

The said decision of the federal agency of executive power for the securities market concerning the suspension (or annulment) of a license issued to a professional participant of the securities market shall enter into force upon the expiry of 15 days from the moment of receipt thereof by the professional participant of the securities market, and in the event of an appeal against the said decision to a court – from the moment of entry into legal force of the decision of the court. The decision of the federal agency of executive power for the securities market shall be considered to be received by the professional participant of the securities market from the moment of handing over a copy of the decision to a representative of the professional participant of the securities market under receipt or upon the expiry of six days from the moment of sending a copy of the decision to the professional participant of the securities market by registered letter [added by Federal Law No. 185-ФЗ, 28 December 2002].

3. With respect to emitents effectuating the emission of securities not in good faith the federal agency of executive power for the securities market shall [as amended by Federal Law No. 185-ФЗ, 28 December 2002]:

take measures to suspend the further placement of securities issued as a result of the emission not in good faith;

publish in the mass media information concerning the fact of the emission not in good faith and the grounds for the suspension of the placement of securities issued as a result of an emission not in good faith;

notify in writing the necessity to eliminate violations, make changes in the securities prospectus and other conditions of the issue, and also establish periods for the elimination of the violations [as amended by Federal Law No. 185-ФЗ, 28 December 2002];

send materials of a verification with regard to the facts of the emission not in good faith to a court for the application of measures of administrative responsibility against officials of the emitent in accordance with legislation of the Russian Federation;

send materials of a verification with regard to the facts of an emission not in good faith to procuracy agencies when there are in the actions of the officials of the emitent the indicia of the constituent elements of a crime;

issue a written directive concerning the authorisation of the further placement of securities in the event of the elimination by the emitent of violations connected with the emission of securities not in good faith;

apply to a court with a suit to deem the issue of securities to be invalid if the emission not in good faith entailed the deluding of possessors having material significance, or if the purposes of the emission are contrary to the foundations of legal order and morality.

4. Officials of the emitent who adopted the decision concerning the issue of securities into circulation which did not undergo State registration shall bear administrative or criminal responsibility in accordance with legislation of the Russian Federation.

5. The issue of securities may be deemed invalid upon the suit of the federal agency of executive power for the securities market, regional divisions of the federal agency of executive power for the securities market, the State registering agency, State tax service agency, procurator, and also the suits of other State agencies effectuating powers in the sphere of the securities market in accordance with legislation of the Russian Federation [as amended by Federal Law No. 185-ФЗ, 28 December 2002].

The deeming of the issue of securities to be invalid shall entail the withdrawal of the securities from circulation which were issued in violation of the established procedure for registration or emission of securities and the return to the possessors of the monetary means (or other property) received by the emitent as payment for the securities.

6. Professional activity on the securities market effectuated without a license shall be illegal.

With respect to the persons effectuating unlicensed activity the federal agency of executive power for the securities market shall [as amended by Federal Law No. 185-ФЗ, 28 December 2002]:

take measures to suspend the unlicensed activity;

publish in the mass media information concerning the fact of unlicensed activity of a participant of the securities market;

notify in writing about the necessity to receive a license, and also establish the periods for this;

send materials of a verification with regard to the facts of unlicensed activity to a court for the application of measures of administrative responsibility against the officials of the participant of the securities market in accordance with legislation of the Russian Federation;

apply to an arbitrazh court with a suit concerning the recovery to the revenue of the State of the revenues received as a result of unlicensed activity on the securities market;

apply to an arbitrazh court with a suit concerning the compulsory liquidation of the participant of the securities market in the event of the failure thereof to receive a license within the established periods.

7. In the event of the discovery of facts of an advertisement not in good faith the federal agency of executive power for the securities market shall [as amended by Federal Law No. 185-ФЗ, 28 December 2002]:

take measures to suspend the advertisement not in good faith;

notify in writing the advertiser about the necessity of terminating the advertisement not in good faith and also establish the periods for this;

publish in the mass media information concerning the facts of the advertisement not in good faith and the advertisers not in good faith;

send materials of a verification with regard to the facts of an advertisement not in good faith to a court for the application of measures of administrative responsibility against officials of a participant of the securities market-advertiser in accordance with legislation of the Russian Federation;

suspend the operation of a license for the effectuation of activity of professional participants of the securities market effectuating the advertisement of securities not in good faith;

apply to a court with a suit concerning the deeming of the issue of securities to be invalid if the advertisement not in good faith entailed the deluding of possessors having material significance.

8. Professional participants of the securities market and emitents of securities, and also their officials, shall have the

right to appeal against the actions of the federal agency of executive power for the securities market with regard to suppressing violation of legislation of the Russian Federation on securities and the application of measures of responsibility in the procedure provided for by legislation of the Russian Federation [as amended by Federal Law No. 185-ФЗ, 28 December 2002].

9. In the instances provided for by the present Federal Law and other legislative acts of the Russian Federation on securities, the participants of the securities market shall be obliged to secure the property interests of the possessors with a pledge, guarantee, and by other means provided for by civil legislation of the Russian Federation, and also to insure the property and risks connected with activity on the securities market.

Article 51¹. Peculiarities of Placement and Circulation of Securities of Foreign Emitents [added by Federal Law No. 185-ФЗ, 28 December 2002]

1. Securities of foreign emitents, except for securities of international financial organisations, admitted for placement and public circulation in the Russian Federation, when there is an international treaty of the Russian Federation or agreement concluded between the federal agency of executive power for the securities market on the basis of a decision of the Government of the Russian Federation and respective agency (or organisation) of the country of the foreign emitent and providing for the procedure of their interaction.

A list of international financial organisations whose securities are admitted for placement and public circulation in the Russian Federation shall be confirmed by the Government of the Russian Federation.

2. In the event of the public placement and/or public circulation of securities of foreign emitents, including interna-

tional financial organisations, the recording of the rights to such securities shall be effectuated by depositaries which are juridical persons in accordance with legislation of the Russian Federation and respective requirements of normative legal acts of the federal agency of executive power for the securities market for such depositaries.

3. Requirements for documents to be submitted for State registration of an issue (or additional issue) of emission securities of foreign emitents, including international financial organisations, for the registration of securities prospectuses and State registration of reports concerning the results of issues (or additional issues) of emission securities of such emitents, the composition of information to be included in these documents, the formalisation thereof, and also the composition of information and procedure for the disclosure of information by foreign emitents, including international financial organisations, shall apply by taking into account exceptions determined by normative legal acts of the federal agency of executive power for the securities market.

Article 52. Transitional Provisions in Connection With Entry into Force of Present Federal Law

Credit organizations shall have the right to effectuate professional activity on the securities market on the basis of a license for the effectuation of banking operations within one year from the entry into force of the present Federal Law. The federal agency of executive power for the securities market shall have the right to extend the said period up to two years [as amended by Federal Law No. 185-Ф3, 28 December 2002].

Investment institutes effectuating professional activity on the securities market on the basis of a license issued before the entry into force of the present Federal Law, and also stock exchanges must bring their constitutive and internal documents (reglaments) into conformity with it within one year from the date of its official publication. The federal agency of executive power for the securities market shall have the right to extend the said period up to two years [as amended by Federal Law No. 185-ФЗ, 28 December 2002].

Article 53. Procedure for Entry into Force of Present Federal Law

1. The present Federal Law shall enter into force from the date of its official publication.
2. To propose to the President of the Russian Federation and charge the Government of the Russian Federation to bring their normative legal acts into conformity with the present Federal Law.